Folktales from Kashmir

Vinita Zutshi is an author, storyteller and transformational parenting coach. She mentors adults and children in creative writing, storytelling and communication. When she's not doing any of the above or reading, she can be found creating puzzles, tending her vegetable patch and speaking in tongues (six, at last count). Find out more at www.vinitazutshi.com.

Published by Red Panda, an imprint of Westland Books, a division of Nasadiya Technologies Private Limited, in 2025

No. 269/2B, First Floor, 'Irai Arul', Vimalraj Street, Nethaji Nagar, Alapakkam Main Road, Maduravoyal, Chennai 600095

Westland, the Westland logo, Red Panda and the Red Panda logo are the trademarks of Nasadiya Technologies Private Limited, or its affiliates.

ISBN: 9789360459727
10 9 8 7 6 5 4 3 2 1

Printed at Saurabh Printers Pvt. Ltd

RED PANDA

Folktales from Kashmir

Vinita Zutshi

Illustrated by Charbak Dipta

For Mona

Contents

Author's Note

As a storyteller, I have told stories to thousands aged two to eighty-seven. Lots of these stories have been folktales, but not a single one was from Kashmir, where my family comes from. It says a lot that this never struck me as odd until I began writing this book.

My Kashmiriyat was of the kind that many Kashmiris can unfortunately relate to—rootless. In my family, we cooked and relished the traditional food but that was my only connection to the culture; partly because we lived all over the country and Koshur wasn't spoken at home; partly because my parents were forward-thinking, and perhaps, to them, that meant letting us be.

With one pair of grandparents focused on a large extended family that held itself aloof, and the other intent on philosophical pursuits, it is only natural that I grew up in cultural hollowness.

It took writing this book to realise that some of this hollowness is shared by more Kashmiris than I thought. No one in my large family has ever heard a folktale from Kashmir in their life despite many of them having been born and raised to adulthood in Srinagar. From my father's childhood to today, the focus for millions of Kashmiris has been on getting a good education, and stories were not part of a good education.

Each story is preceded by an object that is quintessential to being Kashmiri, along with its Koshur pronunciation. May these be a window for you to see into the Kashmiri soul.

My hope is that the stories in this book land in the hollow spaces in our hearts, Kashmiri or not, and help us feel grounded, and more connected to each other. Because each of us is a story, and our stories entwine with each other to make the tree of life.

Folktales from Kashmir

Saffron crocus

'kɒŋ pəʊʃ - its subtle flavour, rich colour and health benefits make saffron valuable, with its labour-intensive picking and small harvest from each flower making it the most expensive spice in the world

The Foolish Man

There was once a man who lived with his wife in a village. He was known throughout the area for being a foolish fellow; nothing could be done about that. But what irritated his wife was that he was also lazy. No matter how often she told him to go out and do something, he would not leave the house. He was content to sit at home and gossip with visitors, eat his meals and 'rest' frequently on his cot.

As time went on, his wife became more and more insistent that he go out to work. 'Open a business of your choice or find a job, but do something. I cannot stand you lazing around the house while I labour all day,' she would say. But besides being foolish and lazy, he was also stubborn. He simply refused to step out of the house. Desperate, she took to nagging him every day but he turned a deaf ear to both her pleas and her threats.

One day, when his wife returned from the market and began criticising him again, he said, 'I have heard that there is a wise old man across the river, sitting under a tree, telling everyone's fortune. I will go and ask him what my future holds.' His wife was so happy that he was getting out of the house with some goal in mind that she bid him farewell without asking him any questions.

The river was quite far from the village, so the man set a steady pace and began walking. The weather was pleasant and since he had not stepped out of the house in many years, he enjoyed looking around at the chinar, apple and walnut trees. Lavender, daisies, buttercups, roses and marigolds grew in profusion, and he inhaled their scents as he passed by. As he left the village behind, he saw someone approaching him. As they got closer to each other, he realised it was a bear. Before he could think of running away and hiding, the bear spoke. 'Where are you coming from, and where are you going?'

The man was so astonished to hear the bear speak that he forgot his fear and answered, 'I'm coming from the village. I have heard there is a wise old man across the river who is telling everyone's fortune. I am going there to find out what is written in my destiny.'

The bear said, 'Since you are going to meet the wise man, please ask him about my fortune as well. I'm having a difficult time: my head aches for six months of the year. And for the remaining six months, I am either asleep or have no energy at all. Ask him why I am in this state, and how I can be cured of my headache and live a full life.'

The man agreed to do so and walked on. It was a long way to the river and he was beginning to have a hollow feeling in his stomach when he came upon a tree laden with fruit. He plucked one and took a large bite but spat it out almost immediately. It was the most

bitter thing he had ever tasted. He threw the fruit away. The moment it landed on the ground, the tree spoke up. 'Where are you coming from and where are you going?'

The man told the tree that he was going to see the wise old man to find out what was in his fate. The tree said, 'Since you will be meeting the wise old man, please ask him a question from me. I am a good tree with a strong trunk and healthy, leafy branches. Then why is my fruit so bitter?'

The man agreed to ask the wise old man the tree's question, and went on his way. After some time, he reached the river. It ran strong and deep, and the opposite bank was far away. He looked for a bridge or boat, but there seemed no way to cross the river. As he stood there thinking of other ways to get across, a large fish popped its head out of the water near his feet and asked him, 'Where are you coming from and where are you going?'

The man told the fish where he was coming from and where he was going. 'But how can I cross the river? And if I don't cross it, how will I meet the wise old man?' he said.

'I will take you across the river,' said the fish, 'but please do me a favour in return. Ask the wise old man why I cannot breathe in water.'

The man agreed to ask the wise man the question, and got on the broad back of the fish. It swam strongly against the current till it reached the opposite bank, where it deposited the man. He walked a short distance till he saw an old man sitting in the shade of a wide, leafy tree. He greeted the old man and said, 'I have come to ask you about what fate has in store for me.' Then he narrated his encounters with the bear, the tree and the fish, and asked the wise man all their questions.

The wise man listened in silence. Then he said, 'I will tell you the answers to the questions asked by the bear, the tree and the fish. As for you, I have only one thing to say: your luck follows you. So go where you will, you will see that your luck is behind you.'

The man was thrilled to hear this. 'My luck walks behind me! That's great!' he said. He bowed to the wise old man and retraced his steps homeward. As he reached the riverbank, he saw the fish waiting for him. He told the fish, 'The wise old man said you cannot breathe underwater because there's a jewel stuck in your throat. Whoever removes this precious stone from your throat will become rich, and once the jewel is removed, you will be able to breathe properly in the water.'

The fish wriggled joyfully. It said, 'Now I know what to do! But where am I going to find a person to take the jewel out of my throat? You are here, and you know everything, so it would be best if you were the one to help me. If you take the jewel out of my throat, you will become wealthy, and I will be able to breathe freely. We will both fulfil our heart's desires.'

The man said, 'No, I don't have the time to take the jewel out of your throat. The wise man told me that my luck follows me, so I'll be on my way so that Lady Luck can follow me all the way home. Right now, can you help me cross the river?'

The fish rose slightly out of the water so the man could get on its back, and swam vigorously to the other bank. The man stepped ashore, thanked the fish and continued homeward. When he reached the fruit-laden tree, he stopped. The branches of the tree trembled in anticipation as they waited to hear the man's words. 'The wise man said there's a large treasure buried under you, and whoever digs it up will become wealthy beyond their wildest dreams. Once the buried treasure is removed, the fruits you bear will be sweet again.'

The tree said, 'That's great! I need someone to dig up the treasure buried under me. If you were to dig it up, you will become rich beyond your wildest dreams, and my fruit will be sweet again.'

The man replied, 'No, I cannot do that. You see, the wise old man told me that my fortune walks behind me, so I am in a hurry to get home. I'm sure you will be able to find someone to dig up the treasure, and your fruit will be sweet again.' He raced homeward. His pace slowed when he saw the bear standing in his path.

The bear asked, 'What did the wise old man tell you?'

The man told the bear about meeting the tree, the fish and the wise man. He told him the wise man's answers to the problems of the fish and the tree, and how his own luck followed in his footsteps. Finally, he narrated how the fish and tree had requested him to help them, but he had been in too much of a hurry to get home, so he had to ask them to look for help elsewhere.

The bear listened to the entire tale patiently and then asked, 'What did the wise man say about my problem?'

The man replied, 'The wise old man said you need to find a stupid person and devour his brain. Doing so will cure your headache for good and keep you healthy and active throughout the year.'

The bear thought about everything the man had said and done. Then he said, 'I am positive that there is no one more foolish than you. You had two opportunities to become the owner of untold wealth and you squandered them both.' Saying this, he swiped one paw across the man's left cheek and another one across his right cheek. The impact of the bear's hefty slaps shook the man's brain out of his head, and the bear gobbled it up immediately.

It is difficult to know whether the wise old man had offered the right solutions to the problems of the bear, the tree and the fish, but he was certainly accurate when it came to the man. His fortune kept following in his footsteps but alas, he was too foolish to make use of it!

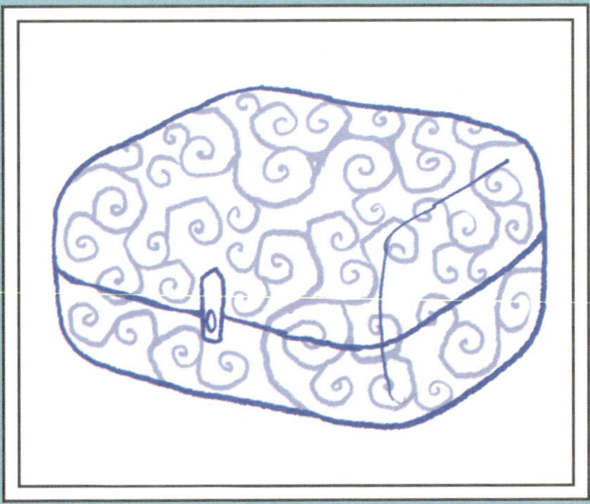

Papier mâché

'peɪpər mæʃeɪ - recycled paper pulp that is shaped into ornate items of home decor, and painted with motifs from the flora and fauna of Kashmir

The Old Woman and the Thieves

An old woman lived alone. She was well-off and her house was filled with beautiful furniture and lovely things; she dressed well and enjoyed a luxurious lifestyle. One evening, she kneaded some dough and made three rotis for herself. But then she realised that she was no longer hungry so she covered them and set the dish aside.

She decided to do her hair, hoping she would feel hungry after that. She had long white hair, and she was particular about combing it well every night. She made sections of her hair, combing through each section dozens of times. As a result, her hair flowed down all over her head and no part of her face or neck could be seen. After some time, she grew tired and stopped combing, thinking about her dinner.

Unnoticed by her, three thieves arrived just then, planning to burgle her house. They crept quietly and crouched against the outside wall of the house, under an open window. One of them stood up a little to peek through the window to see what was happening inside. By chance, he happened to look into the room where the old woman was doing her hair.

He saw a figure with white hair all over its head and he heard the figure say, 'I'll eat two today and one tomorrow.'

The thief was shaken. They had scoped the house so carefully. An old woman lived alone in it, and they had crept up to the house so stealthily. Still, the old woman had managed to find out that there were three of them. Moreover, she was planning to eat them!

He sat back down, and in rapid gestures and whispers, told the other two thieves that it would be best for them to leave and look for some other house to loot. 'I don't know how, but she knows about us, and is planning to eat two of us today and the third one tomorrow!' he said.

The thief who thought himself the bravest of them all said with contempt, 'Stop making excuses and just say that you're scared of a lonely old woman. Let me take a look.' Then he stood up and peeped through the window.

He saw a strange figure with no face and silver hair falling all over its head. The figure moved and said, 'I'll eat one today and two tomorrow. Yes, that would be better.'

The brave thief fell on top of the others. When his heartbeat had calmed a little, he said, 'We have made a mistake. The one who lives here is not an old woman but a *rantas*. She only shows her true form at night, when there is no one around to see her. Being a rantas, it is no surprise that she knows we are here. I think we had better vamoose from here before she gobbles us up.' Suiting the action to the word, they ran away as fast as they could.

Meanwhile, the old woman who was used to talking to herself because she lived alone, said again, 'Yes, I'll eat one today and two tomorrow.' Then she tied her hair in a bun and reached for the roti she had decided to eat then, leaving the other two for the next day.

Lotus

pʌm'pəʊʃ - a sacred symbol of Lord Shiva, it is also a food source; its seeds are a snack and its stem, a popular vegetable

The Jackal, the Rooster and the Rabbit

A rooster and a rabbit were good friends and often spent time together. One day, as they were chatting in a field, a jackal spotted them from a distance. His mouth watered at the sight of these animals. If only he could find a way to eat them without tiring himself by having to chase and hunt them down! He thought for some time. When he had hatched a plan, he smiled and licked his lips. He began walking slowly towards them, making no attempt to hide his approach.

The moment the rooster and rabbit saw the jackal coming towards them, they turned to run. Immediately, the jackal called out to them. His voice rang out faint but clear. 'Brothers! I come in peace. I want to be your friend. I have killed many animals in the past and have decided to atone for my sins. I have prayed to God for forgiveness. As a mark of my repentance, I have made a solemn vow not to kill another living being. Not only that, I have also decided to abstain from eating meat. My deepest desire is to spend a pious life devoted to the Lord. Brothers, you are in no danger from me. On the contrary, I want to be friends with you.'

On hearing these unexpected words from the jackal, the rooster and the rabbit stopped in their tracks and turned to face him. As the jackal walked towards them, he kept repeating his words, reassuring them that all he wanted was to be friends with them.

The rabbit turned to the rooster and said, 'It sounds like this jackal is really sorry for all the wicked things he's done.'

The jackal continued to shout. 'Brothers, believe it or not, I just passed a large chicken coop. Earlier, I would have grabbed one of the hens in my jaws, leaving the others squawking, flapping and running to save themselves from me. But this time? This time, I simply walked past without even looking at the hens and chickens. And that's only because I am trying to show how truly sorry I am for all the wrongs I have committed, the blood I have shed. All I want to do now is to atone for my sins.'

As he came closer, he reduced his volume so they wouldn't be deafened. With his last words, the jackal came right up to where the rooster and the rabbit were standing.

They greeted each other. The jackal suggested that they sit down and said, 'Brothers, you know about the evil deeds I have committed. It is only fair that you tell me about your sins as well. We will recount our sins and ask God for forgiveness.'

He turned towards the rabbit and said, 'Brother Rabbit, let's start with you. List all the sins you are guilty of so we can count them.'

For a while, there was silence as the rabbit tried to remember, going far back into the past to identify his sins. Suddenly, he straightened up, saying, 'Got it! Once, I found a field of carrots. Every day, early in the morning, I would uproot two of the carrots, munch on them and disappear long before the farmer appeared in the field. This went on for months. I must have eaten hundreds of carrots.' His face fell as he added, 'I mean, I must have *stolen* hundreds of carrots.'

The jackal thundered, 'Brother Rabbit! That's a terrible, terrible crime! It is such a bad crime that you will never be able to make amends for it by simply asking for forgiveness. Only a suitable punishment will absolve you of your sins.' Turning to the rooster, the jackal continued, 'Brother Rooster, you decide what Brother Rabbit's punishment should be.'

The rooster stared at the jackal, then looked at the ground and mumbled, 'Me? How can I say what his punishment should be?'

The jackal was furious. He thundered, 'Very well then, I will decide!' He looked into the frightened rabbit's eyes and said, 'You don't have the right to live, Brother Rabbit! You have taken the hard-earned fruits of a farmer's labour without even thinking of giving anything in return. Since you have not respected the hard work of another, you have forfeited the right to live.' Saying this, he reached for the rabbit and wrung his neck.

The rooster trembled when he saw the rabbit's lifeless body.

The jackal looked at the rooster and said, 'Brother Rooster! It is your turn now. List your sins. Tell me, what wrongs have you done?'

The rooster was so nervous that he could not speak. A large lump seemed to be stuck in his throat. He tried to swallow it down and stammered, 'N– n– no, I haven't done anything wrong in my entire life. I am completely innocent. All I do is peck at a few grains throughout the day. That is all I do.'

The jackal refused to accept this answer. 'You must have done something wrong, you must have sinned. You *must* have. It is not possible that you have never sinned. There is nobody on earth who has never sinned. Think hard and tell me: how have you sinned?'

The rooster's brain was almost paralysed with fright, but he realised that he could not risk angering the jackal. He took a deep breath and forced himself to go over his life, trying to find something he could confess to. When at last he recalled an incident, relief flooded his voice. 'Ah! I remember now. Once, I had strayed from my coop and entered the courtyard of a neighbour, where wheat was spread out in the sun on a sheet. The sea of wheat was tempting, and I started pecking at the grains. I had barely eaten four or five of them when a woman came out of the house and shooed me away. This is the only wrong thing I remember having done in my life.'

The jackal fixed the rooster with a stern gaze. 'I see! Even you have taken advantage of a farmer's labour! Do you even know the immense value of what you have plundered?' He bellowed, 'Even you don't have the right to live after having committed such an appalling act!' He reached for the rooster and killed it.

Saliva pooled in the wily jackal's mouth as he saw the two animals he had so cleverly 'hunted'. He congratulated himself and began to eat.

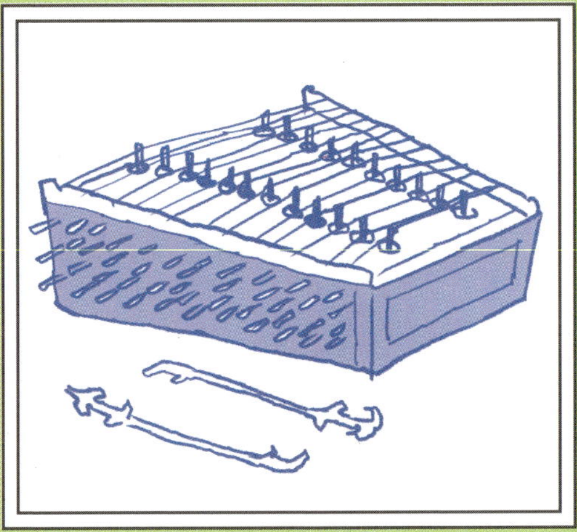

Santoor

sʌn'tuːr - a traditional musical instrument with one hundred strings, used to play folk music and sufi music

Jabba and Nabba

There were two brothers called Jabba and Nabba. Jabba, the younger of the two, spent his time sleeping, eating and chatting with whoever he could find.

Nabba worked hard all day, and earned enough money to support his family as well as that of his idle brother. Every day he thought he would ask Jabba to find a job for himself, but every day he shrank from the unpleasantness of getting into an argument with his brother. He tried to hint to Jabba that he should earn his livelihood, but all his suggestions fell on deaf ears.

Years passed and the situation remained the same. One day, Nabba couldn't tolerate his brother's laziness any longer and told him that from then on, the families would live separately. 'You should find some work so that you can earn a livelihood and support your family,' he told Jabba before he moved out.

Forced to earn a living, Jabba set out to look for a job. But every place he went to ask for a job, he was asked what experience he had. When he told them that he didn't have any experience, some people laughed at him, others threw him out, while yet others made fun of him. 'You have spent so many years on earth—you must have been doing something with your time. How can you have no experience?'

Jabba may have had no work experience, but he knew that telling people that he had spent all his time sleeping, eating and chatting would not help him find a job. And so he continued his search. One day, he met a *khwaja* who was looking for a servant. Jabba approached him timidly, expecting to be asked about his skills and experience. But to his surprise and joy, the khwaja asked no such questions. 'So! You want to work for me as my personal servant? You look healthy and strong. I'll hire you. Stay with me at my house and do what I ask you to do. I will pay your salary at the end of the month.'

Jabba agreed and they reached an agreement.

'But I have one condition,' continued the khwaja.

Jabba, who had never worked a day in his life, did not understand what it meant to work under a condition. But since he was desperate for work, he said, 'Please tell me what your condition is.'

The khwaja said, 'If one of us gets angry with the other, the one who gets angry will have his nose cut off.'

Jabba had no idea what this meant but agreed to it because he needed to feed his family.

The next morning was his first day at work. At daybreak, the khwaja told Jabba to take his oxen and plough, and plough one of his fields. He gave precise directions so Jabba could locate the field. As Jabba was leaving with the plough and oxen, the khwaja added, 'Mind that you plough the entire field well, and after you finish, bring back some greens and food for the cooking pot in the evening. Also get some wood for the stove.'

Jabba agreed and left for the field. When he saw how large it was, his heart sank. He had never done any work before, but he knew that he had to begin now so he gathered his scattered wits and started. Naturally, no matter how hard he worked, he was both slow and inefficient, and by sunset, he had barely ploughed half the field. As he made his way back to the khwaja's house with the plough and oxen, he thought, 'It is already very late. Where will I find wood for the fire and food for the cooking pot? Surely the khwaja will understand.'

The moment he entered the house, the khwaja asked him, 'Where is the wood and what have you brought as food?'

Jabba could not believe what he was hearing. Chest heaving with fury, he said, 'Khwaja *sahab*, what are you saying? You can see that my clothes and hands are stained with dirt. You can see that I am so tired from ploughing the field that I can barely stand upright or keep my eyes open. Where do you think I could have had the time or energy to bring any wood or food? Be reasonable.'

The khwaja said, 'Oh! You have got angry at my words. In the morning, you agreed that after ploughing the field you would bring wood for the fire and food for the cooking pot. Now you're going back on your word. Moreover, remember that you agreed to my condition that if one of us gets angry, his nose will be cut off. Don't say I didn't warn you!' Saying this, the khwaja reached for a sharp knife and cut off Jabba's nose.

Blood gushed from Jabba's nose and he howled in pain. Holding the edge of his *pheran* to his nose to stem the flow of blood, he staggered home, where he collapsed. His wife started screaming when she saw Jabba's bloodied face, and sent for Nabba, who rushed over.

Nabba took one look at the injured man and exploded. 'Tell me, my brother, who has done this evil deed?'

Jabba narrated the entire tale of woe, beginning with his happiness at finding a job with the khwaja and ending with the khwaja cutting off his nose.

Nabba's eyes glittered as he heard the crafty khwaja's condition. 'Don't worry, little brother. Get some rest, recover your health and energy. I will teach this khwaja a lesson he will never forget.'

The next morning, Nabba set off for the khwaja's house, pretending to look for employment.

'I need someone to work in my house because there is a lot of work to be done,' said the khwaja, 'but first, you need to agree to a condition. If one of us gets angry, his nose will be cut off. Do you agree?'

Nabba agreed and was immediately taken into the khwaja's service.

In the morning, the khwaja gave him the same task he had given Jabba. 'Take the plough and my oxen and go to my field, the one that's next to the mountain stream. Plough the entire field well, and after you finish, bring some wood for the stove and some food to put in the cooking pot. Now go!'

Nabba said, 'Khwaja sahab, I will do everything you've asked me to do. Not only that, I am also taking your sheep so they can graze. I will keep an eye on them.' He hefted the plough onto his shoulders, picked up the lead ropes of the oxen, a staff to herd the sheep, and left. He had spent his entire life working, so he knew what to do, and was efficient at it. He ploughed the field till the soil was well tilled. It was sunset when he finished. Now that it was time to go back, he turned his mind to the khwaja's other tasks.

First, he needed wood for the stove. He found it easily by chopping up the wooden plough into sticks of kindling which he tied into a bundle using a reed growing by the stream. Next he needed to find food for the evening meal. That was simple too. He slaughtered one of the sheep, cut its meat, and made another bundle. When he reached the khwaja's house, he called out loudly.

'Khwaja sahab, look! I have brought wood for the fire and meat for the pot.'

The khwaja was amazed and delighted to hear Nabba's words. In all his life, this was the first time a servant had fulfilled all his requests. He resolved to treat his hard-working servant well. He approached Nabba with a huge smile on his face. 'Show me what you've got!'.

Nabba showed him the bundle of kindling and said, 'As you know, I was hard at work all day tilling the field. I had no time to fetch wood for the stove, so I chopped up the plough for firewood. Here it is! And I killed one of your sheep so you could have meat for the evening meal. The other three are back in the barn.'

The khwaja's face turned red. He shook his fist at Nabba and thundered, 'You fool! What have you done?'

Nabba said, 'Watch out, Khwaja sahab! You've got angry!' With one quick movement he reached for the knife that hung on his belt, and cut off the khwaja's nose. As the injured man fell to the floor, Nabba looked at him and continued, 'Did you think that you could cut off my brother's nose and not answer for it? That you would get away scot-free without taking any responsibility? That nobody would avenge him?'

With these words, he turned his back on the mutilated khwaja and walked home, pleased at having avenged Jabba.

Guchhi

'kʌngʊchh - used in pulao, these mushrooms are said to grow spontaneously when a certain type of lightning strikes the ground. They grow in a line that can go on for miles, and it is said that only a dark person can find them.

The Farmer's Bullock

A farmer had a pair of oxen that he would yoke together to plough his field. They were strong cattle and worked well together, and the farmer was very proud of them. One day, an accident befell one of the oxen and it died. The farmer was grief-stricken. Not only had he lost an animal he was fond of, but he was also worried that he would not be able to plough the field and ply his trade with only one ox.

He went to the *zamindar* who owned the field and told him about the tragedy. The zamindar said, 'I'm willing to loan you one hundred rupees. You can use the money to buy another ox, and then you can carry on farming.'

The farmer agreed and went looking for a healthy animal to pair up with his ox. After many days' search, he arrived in a village where he found a strong young bullock who would be a good match for his ox. This bullock had not yet attained full maturity, but it would grow into a fine animal. It was the best animal the farmer had seen thus far, and he decided to buy it. He offered the owner one hundred rupees for the bullock, and a bargain was struck. Thrilled, the farmer led the bullock away, back to his own village.

On the way, he met a muscular young man who asked, 'Where are you coming from and where are you going?'

The farmer said, 'One of my oxen died, so I've been looking to buy a bullock. I finally found this prize specimen, so I bought it and now I'm heading back home.' He smiled with satisfaction as he looked at his bullock.

The man said, '*Arre*! What are you saying? This is a dog! Where did you buy this dog?'

The farmer said, 'What is wrong with you? Why are you calling my bullock a dog? Looks like you've never seen an ox before, that's why you can't tell the difference between an ox and a dog.'

The man looked like he wanted to argue further but the farmer held up his hand indicating that he did not want to hear any more about it, and led his bullock onward.

After he had walked a couple of miles, a man sitting under a tree hailed him. '*Bhaisahab*! Where are you taking this dog? Where have you got it from, and why are you leading it like this?'

The farmer was taken aback. He replied, 'You are ignorant. This is an ox, not a dog. What is wrong with the people of this village that they think an ox is a dog?'

The man said, 'Bhaisahab, why are you getting angry? All I've done is to call a dog a dog. Surely

there's nothing wrong with that! What makes you think this is a bullock? I can see quite clearly that this is a dog.'

The farmer left in a huff. As he walked, he looked back at the bullock he had purchased. He stopped and walked all around it, inspecting it carefully. Yes, it had horns, hooves, a tail. Of course it was a bullock! And it should be! He had bought a bullock after all. Why were these people calling it a dog? 'Very peculiar people,' he concluded, calmed himself, and resumed walking.

After about a mile, a man sitting by the roadside shouted, 'Brother, where did you buy this dog? And where are you taking it? That's a really good dog you've got there. It looks a lot like a bullock.'

The farmer stood still. 'What is going on?' he thought. 'Is this really a dog? No, no. I know I bought an ox. How can it be a dog?' He looked at the animal again. It looked like an ox, but he was beginning to doubt the evidence of his own eyes. 'No, it cannot be a dog,' he muttered to himself and walked on. He was very close to his home now and quickened his footsteps.

He met an old man coming from the opposite direction. The old man looked pious, God-fearing, and wise, like an elder. He had a long beard, wore white clothes, and had a white shawl draped over his shoulders. The old man's footsteps slowed as he came close to the farmer. He said, 'Son, where have you got this dog from? It's a very nice dog, it looks just like an ox. Why are you leading it? Did you catch it somewhere?'

The farmer was now convinced that there was something wrong with his eyesight. This pious old man had no reason to bamboozle him. The three brawny fellows he had met earlier could well have been ruffians out to cheat him, but the old man had no reason to lie to him. It was clear that he had inadvertently bought a dog instead of a bullock. What was the point of leading a dog home? He let go of the rope he had been holding and walked home, empty-handed.

As soon as he disappeared from sight, the three men who had spoken to him earlier, who had been following the farmer without his knowing it, came out onto the road. The old man grabbed the rope, and together, they led the bullock away. The four men were actually a gang of thieves who had developed different stratagems to cheat people of their belongings. And this is how they made a fool of the farmer and stole his bullock.

Shikara

ʃɪ'kara - wooden boat used to transport people and goods across rivers and lakes

The Weak Brother

There were once three brothers who lived with their wives in one house, even though they owned three houses together. The two older brothers were robust and strong but the youngest was thin and weak. They worked together, but the older two managed to get their youngest brother to do most of the work.

One day, they decided to live in separate households. The older two picked well-constructed houses and left the youngest with the house that was so dilapidated that it would not be an exaggeration to call it broken down. Then it was time to divide the buffaloes. Once again, the two older brothers took the healthy, sturdy buffaloes, leaving the youngest with the buffalo that was just skin and bone. When he protested, the oldest brother told him that he was getting the weak buffalo because he himself was also skin and bone. The older brothers divided the furniture and other household items in the same way, leaving the most worn out and broken things for the youngest. They also owned one field with lush grass, where the buffaloes grazed. The oldest brother said, 'I am the eldest, so I will keep this field.'

When everything was divided, the youngest brother looked at his ramshackle house which was in desperate need of repair, and at his feeble buffalo, and turned to his wife sadly. 'What are we to do now?'

His wife said, 'Don't despair. Your brother may not have allowed us to use his field, but there is more than enough grass there. We will take our buffalo there every night, when there will be no one to see her. She will graze her fill and become strong again. And we will bring her back before dawn so that nobody finds out.' Her advice proved sound, for in a few weeks, the buffalo looked completely different from the bag of bones that had been given to the weak brother.

The older brothers noticed the difference and decided to keep an eye on their younger sibling and his buffalo. One evening, they saw him taking the buffalo somewhere under cover of darkness. They followed. When they saw that the buffalo was grazing in the oldest brother's field of grass, they were furious. They waited for the youngest brother to leave and then killed the buffalo.

When the weak brother and his wife went to the field just before dawn to bring the buffalo back, they saw that it was dead. They burst into tears. He said, 'What can we do now?'

His wife said, 'Let us skin the buffalo, clean its hide and try to sell it in the market. Who knows, we might get some money for it.'

The weak brother took the hide to the market and spent all day trying to sell it, but nobody was interested in buying it. He waited so long that it was dark by the time he bent his steps homeward. There was a jungle between the market and his home. When he reached the jungle, he realised it was too dark to walk through it. He looked for a tall tree and decided to sleep on one of its branches with the buffalo skin spread under him to provide a slight cushion. Since he was tired, he fell asleep quickly.

At some time in the night, a sound woke him. He peered down through the leaves and saw three thieves sitting at the foot of the tree. They were arguing about how to divide their loot, and one of them began to threaten the others. The weak brother was so frightened that he wet his pants before he even realised it. The pee fell onto the buffalo skin and dripped onto some stones at the foot of the tree. When the thieves heard something fall drop by drop, they stopped arguing immediately. Afraid that someone had found them and was about to catch them, they abandoned the gold they had stolen and ran away. In the morning, when the weak brother got down from the tree, he saw all the gold the thieves had left behind. He gathered it up and took it home.

He used the money sensibly. First, he repaired his house, plugging all the leaks, reinforcing the foundations and walls and so on until the house stood strong, freshly painted and proud. Next, he bought a strong buffalo. His older brothers observed these developments with disbelief. When they could no longer hold back their curiosity, they confronted him and demanded, 'Where did you get all this wealth?'

He replied, 'I sold the buffalo skin in the market and got a good price for it. These days, people pay well for a good buffalo skin.'

The two brothers promptly killed their buffaloes, skinned them and headed to the market. They hawked their skins from morning to night but did not find a single person interested in buying them. When they got back, they went first to the weak brother's house.

'You lied to us. Tell us how you got your wealth,' they demanded. 'Nobody even looked at the buffalo skins we were selling. Tell us the truth this time: how did you get the money to fix this house and buy a new buffalo? Tell us or else–'

But however much they asked or threatened the weak brother, he stayed silent. Incensed, they burnt his newly renovated house to the ground and left.

The weak brother and his wife railed at their misfortune, but that did nothing but relieve their feelings. All they had left now was a mound of ash. They looked at each other, and the weak brother said, 'Maybe I can sell the ash—' He did not complete the sentence—he knew that he would not find a buyer for ash. Still, they put the ash into a sack to take it to the market. But before they closed the sack, the weak brother took a few coins out of his pocket and put them right at the bottom of the sack.

When he reached the market, he did not try to sell the ash. Instead, he left the sack with a shopkeeper and went to find work that would pay him enough to buy a meal for himself and his wife. He returned to the shop after a couple of hours and began shouting, 'Look! Look! I had left a sack of money here, and someone has taken all the money and left me ash instead. I am ruined! I am ruined! Look at what has happened! Oh! Oh!'

Soon, a crowd gathered around him. 'Have you lost your mind?' one person asked, looking into the sack which the weak brother held open. 'There is nothing but ash in this sack. What do you mean it was full of coins? How can there be coins in a sack full of ash?'

Another man snatched the sack from the weak brother and said, 'I'll show you!' He overturned the sack. Out tumbled the ash, and people had begun to laugh at him when, right at the end, a few coins also fell out. There was a shocked silence after which everyone agreed that the sack must definitely have contained coins before some unscrupulous person took them away and replaced them with ash. The man was right—he had been cheated! But there was no way to find out who the culprit was. The shopkeepers felt bad that such a thing had happened in their market.

They were also ashamed that they had made fun of the weak brother and not believed him at first. So each of them contributed some money so that the weak brother's sack would be full of coins once more.

When he returned from the market, his older brothers were lying in wait for him. They insisted he open the sack and show them what it contained. 'Where did you get all this money from?'

'These days ash fetches a lot of money in the market. I got this money by selling ash.'

The brothers immediately set fire to their own houses and the next day, when the ash had cooled off, they stuffed it into sacks and took it to the market. Obviously, they couldn't get any buyer to take even one

sack of ash from them, even for free. In the evening, they challenged their weak brother in his courtyard. 'You have not been telling us the truth. Tell us, where did you get the sack of coins from? Also, we listened to you and burnt down our houses. Now we have nowhere to live. We don't even have our buffaloes. How will we live? You should share the money with us.'

The weak brother agreed to share his money with them. He said, 'I will give you gold. Whatever you pick up is yours.' Saying this, he threw a handful of gold coins on the ground. The brothers rushed to pick up the coins and then began arguing with each other.

'You have taken more coins than I did. Give me some!' said the eldest brother.

'No, you've taken more so *you* should give me some coins,' protested the younger of the two.

The argument continued, getting more heated as it went on. Finally, the oldest brother was so infuriated that he picked up a rock and hit the second brother on the head with it, killing him. The oldest brother was promptly arrested and put in prison for murder.

And that is how the weak brother became free of his two rascally older brothers.

Kani Shawl

ˈkəŋɪ ʃa:l - coloured pashmina wools on wooden sticks are woven by hand into pashmina yarns of a base colour to create unique shawls

The Bald Man and the Gang of Thieves

Four intelligent thieves had been looting homes and shops in the city without getting caught. Citizens were paralysed with fear because of the thieves' activities—it seemed like there was no way to end the menace of these robbers.

In the same city lived an old woman who had a son who was bald even though he was a young man. He was, like all bald characters in Kashmiri folktales, both witty and cunning. One day he told his mother, 'I am so sharp that I can catch the four thieves who have committed such daring thefts.'

His mother said, 'My bald one, why do you want to invite trouble? These thieves have had the city and all its residents in an uproar. It's best if you don't tangle with them. Let them be and get on with your own life.'

But the bald man was determined to prove his point. 'Ma, just wait and see how I get the better of them. I will put a stop to their thievery. Give me your permission and your blessing that I be successful in what I've undertaken.' His mother argued and pleaded but he refused to listen to her. In the end, she let him go with a heavy heart.

Her warnings echoing in his ears, he left the house and wandered through the nooks and crannies, the narrow lanes and dead-end alleys of the city, looking for the thieves. Late one night, when nobody was about, he turned a corner and finally saw them. The thieves also spotted his bald pate shining from afar as

he came towards them. One of them shouted, 'Hey, baldie! What do you want? Are you tired of living? Do you want to die? Why are you coming towards us?'

The bald man kept walking towards them. When he reached them, he folded his hands and said, 'Brothers, I also want to become a thief. Please include me in your gang. In fact, I will live with you as your slave and learn from you.' In those days, slavery was common. People were bought and sold just like things, and nobody found it odd. The bald man added, 'Moreover, I can also help you on your raids. I possess many skills. If you allow me into your gang, you will be able to loot more people and more valuables from each person. I know many well-to-do people in the city, so I can tell you which homes have more riches so that we can make each raid more profitable. I also know the opportune time to loot each house, since I know when the owners will be away and for how long. Let me join you and you will profit greatly from my being a part of your gang.' He was polite and insistent.

The thieves thought it would be useful to include him in their gang. He could take care of menial tasks, and it would be very agreeable to have a slave at hand.

And they were four to his one–what harm could he possibly do them? So they agreed and the man joined their gang.

The bald man had not been lying. He knew which homes had wealth hidden, and freely shared his knowledge with the gang so that each of their raids was much more profitable and far less risky than it had been earlier. Slowly, he gained the trust of the thieves and began to be accepted as a full member of the gang. After that, they freely shared with him information about all their hideouts and caches.

One day the bald man told them, 'Today, I will be taking you to another city to commit robberies. I have already explored that city thoroughly and am familiar with all its streets and buildings so we should be able to mastermind and pull off some really phenomenal thefts.'

They agreed and set off for the other city. Unknown to the others, the bald man had got some silver melted and commissioned a jeweller to make four thick, heavy silver hoops. He carried these hoops, wrapped in cloth so they would not make a noise, in his pockets as they left the city. When they reached the other city, the man showed them the first house they were to rob. The family that lived in it was away, and the house was within a large compound with high walls so the neighbours would not be able to see or hear the gang as they broke in. The thieves were impressed.

'Let me go in first,' said the bald man, 'and I'll tell you when to come in.' They agreed, and he broke open the latch on a window and entered. Once inside, he took the four silver hoops out of his pocket and counted to twenty. Outside, the thieves were getting restless, wondering why they had to wait outside when there was such a big house waiting to be looted. Just as they were preparing to go in through the window, the bald man came out.

He said, 'Brothers, I have found something so valuable that if we take it to a *saraf*, we will become rich beyond our wildest dreams. So rich that we won't ever need to steal anything again throughout our lives. Look!' He held out the hoops for the thieves to inspect. They saw four large and heavy silver hoops and handled them in wonder.

The four thieves were impressed by the bald man's words. He seemed to know a lot about silver jewellery, and they had complete faith in him so they decided to follow his lead. They said, 'What are these things called?'

He replied, 'These are called *aap char* (you four). There are four of them, so they are called aap char.'

The next day, the leader of the gang said, 'We are new to this city, and you seem to know it well, so you decide which saraf we should take the silver jewellery to.'

The bald man said, 'It will look shady if all of us go looking for a saraf. We are all strangers in this city, and people might suspect us of some wrongdoing. Why don't you all wait here while I find the right saraf for us to approach?'

They agreed and settled under the shade of a tree. 'The market is right here, and you will be able to see me all the time, so don't worry about anything,' the bald man said, and left.

He found a saraf a short distance away and showed him the hoops. The saraf said, 'These are very unusual but I can see that these are hoops, right?'

'No, in our language, we call them aap char.'

'Okay, I will buy your hoops,' said the saraf.

The bald man said, 'That is good, but I also want to sell those four men sitting under that tree. They are my slaves, and I would like to sell them too.'

'Very well,' said the saraf, 'but first, I need to check whether they really are your slaves. I also need to get their consent—would they be willing to work for another master? There's no point buying a slave if he isn't going to work well.'

'Of course,' said the bald man. 'It is understandable that you need to verify these things. Please come with me.' He led the saraf towards the gang sitting under the tree.

The saraf addressed the four men. 'Brothers, I want to buy aap char (you four). Are you four (aap char) ready? Do you agree?'

'Yes, absolutely!' they said enthusiastically. 'You can take aap char right now.'

Smiling broadly, the saraf turned back to his shop with the bald man and paid him a good price for the silver hoops and the four slaves. The man waited for an opportune moment when the thieves' attention was turned away from him, and slipped away, leaving the city by a different route to the one he had used while entering it.

The next thing the thieves knew, the saraf, accompanied by some people, came towards them. As they began tying up the gang members with ropes, the thieves protested loudly, 'Brothers, why are you tying us? What have we done? We have done nothing. We have just been sitting peacefully under a tree.'

The saraf said, 'What are you saying? Your owner has sold you and left. I came with him and asked if you had any objection to my buying you four (aap char), and you agreed. You even told me I could take you four (aap char) right away. Now you are protesting? This is not right.' His men led the four thieves away, not listening to another word they had to say.

As for the bald man, he returned safely to his city. A few days later, he hired a mule and discreetly visited each place where the gang had hidden their loot, taking it away with himself. When he had emptied their entire cache from all their hideouts, he showed the jewels, gold and silver to his mother and told her how he had outwitted the dreaded gang of thieves.

Kanger

'ka:ŋgər - a wicker basket with a handle, which holds an earthen pot that is filled with live coals, it is worn under the *pheran* to keep warm in winter

The Ambitious Old Woman

An old woman who lived alone found an egg in her front yard and kept it carefully in a bin of corn. When she opened the bin a few months later, she found that a rooster had hatched from it. The rooster sprang out, and walked up and down the courtyard. The old woman was delighted to have some company at last, and took good care of the rooster. Inevitably, he took on the role of her son.

One day, as the rooster was pecking the ground for food, he came upon something shiny. He scratched it hard with his claws and found that it was a coin. He ran to the old woman.

'Look, Ma,' he said, 'I found a coin in the yard.'

The old woman told him to take the coin and buy some groceries with it. At the shop, the rooster gave the coin to the merchant and asked for *haldi*, tea leaves, sugar and other supplies. The shopkeeper weighed out everything one at a time and started putting the packages into a bag. As he was putting one of the items into the bag, the coin slipped from his hand and fell into the bag but neither he nor the rooster noticed this. Delighted with his purchases, the rooster carried the bag home.

When the old woman began emptying the bag to put away the groceries, she was surprised to find the coin there. She asked the rooster why he had not paid for the groceries. He replied that he had handed the coin to the shopkeeper and had no idea how it had found its way back into the bag.

'What do you want me to do with the coin?' he asked.

The old woman thought that the rooster might have found a lucky coin. After all, it should have been spent buying groceries, but it had somehow come back to her. She wanted to see how far her luck would go.

'Take this coin to the king,' she said, 'and tell him to give you his daughter's hand in marriage.'

The rooster didn't know any better so he set off for the palace, excited that the coin would help him marry the princess of the land. Lost in happy daydreams, he got a rude shock when he collided with something. When he regained his balance, he saw that a jackal was barring his way.

'Today is my lucky day!' proclaimed the jackal. 'My prey has walked right up to me. Now I will make a meal of you.'

'You can't,' said the rooster. 'I am on my way to meet the king. You see, I wish to marry his daughter. Just let me marry her, and you can eat me after that.'

The jackal thought about it for a while and agreed. 'Take me with you,' he said.

The rooster hid the jackal in his feathers, and walked on. After a while, he encountered a burning lamp.

'Where are you going?' demanded the lamp. 'I won't let you pass. I will burn you.'

'No, please don't. I'm on my way to the king's palace where I will ask for the hand of the princess. After I have married her, I will come back this way, and then you can do whatever you would like to do.'

'But what if you don't come back this way? How can I burn you then?' asked the lamp. 'Take me with you.'

The rooster agreed and hid the lamp in his ear.

When the rooster reached the palace grounds, he called out, 'Your Majesty! Your Highness! Please grant me the hand of your daughter in marriage. I've brought the *meher*.'

The king was busy conducting the affairs of the court when the rooster's voice interrupted him.

'Who is so insolent as to demand the hand of my daughter in marriage by shouting at me from the courtyard?' he asked his courtiers. They sent a sentry to see who it was.

'It's a rooster, *Badshah sahab*!' reported the sentry.

The king could not believe his ears.

'Grab him and put him in the hen coop with the other hens and roosters!' he ordered, and the sentry rushed to obey.

After the sentry had locked the door of the coop and left, the rooster took the jackal from his wing and let it loose in the henhouse. The jackal could not believe his luck. He had spared the life of one rooster, and as a result, he could stuff himself with an entire coop of birds! He proceeded to kill all the birds and eat only the choicest portions of their flesh. When the coop was opened the next morning, not a single hen was found alive. As the farmer with the chicken feed gaped at the bodies strewn around the henhouse, the rooster strolled out to the palace courtyard.

Again he called out, 'Your Majesty! Your Highness! Please marry your daughter off to me. I've brought the meher.'

The king, annoyed at being woken from his slumber, and at what was being demanded, ordered that the rooster be thrown into the cattle pen where the cows and buffaloes would trample him under their hooves. But inside the cattle pen, the rooster let the jackal out of his wing again. In the morning, when the men came to milk the animals, they found that most of the cattle were either injured or dead.

Once again, the rooster took advantage of the commotion to slip out of the pen and make his way to the palace courtyard. Once more he addressed the king. 'Your Highness! Your Majesty! Please let me marry your daughter. I've brought the meher.'

Enraged, the king ordered that the rooster be locked on the roof. 'Maybe an eagle or vulture will eat him, or he might just die of hunger and thirst.'

Alone on the roof, the rooster took the lamp out of his ear and said, 'Do your job now, lamp.'

With a whoosh the lamp blazed till the roof was engulfed in fire. Everything on the roof was destroyed. Hours later, when sentries were sent to neighbouring buildings to see what had become of the rooster, they came back saying that he was hale and hearty but that the roof had been destroyed by fire.

The council of ministers had a hasty consultation and told the king, 'This rooster is more dangerous than we imagined. We have been wracking our brains but have not been able to come up with a way to stop him for good. What can we do?'

'We have to find a way to get rid of him,' said the king. After thinking for a while, he ordered that his

daughter be made ready for the wedding, and invited the rooster into the palace.

The rooster strutted in and handed the coin to the king, saying, 'Please accept this meher for your daughter.'

The king took the coin and said, 'I consent to your marrying my daughter. Come, have some refreshments before we prepare you for the wedding ceremony.'

The rooster settled comfortably on the silk cushions while servers offered him choice delicacies from the royal kitchens. Then he was dressed as a bridegroom and taken to the wedding pavilion. He saw his bride, decked in red and gold, with a *ghunghat* covering her face. After the wedding, it was time for the rooster to take his bride home. A decorated *tanga* stood at the threshold, and the newlyweds were shown into it with great care. They left, the blessings of the king and courtiers echoing in their ears.

'Ma, I have married the princess!' crowed the rooster when the tanga reached the old woman's house. 'I have brought her with me. Come, see your daughter-in-law!'

The old woman could not believe her ears. The coin had indeed been lucky. Now her son would be the king's son-in-law and would eventually sit on the throne, and she would be the future queen's mother-in-law. She opened an old tin trunk to take out a gold bangle, the only thing of value she owned. She had to welcome her daughter-in-law into her new home and perform the ritual of *meher uthana*, where she would lift the bride's veil and give her the gold bangle after seeing her face. The rooster was also eager to see what his bride looked like.

When the old woman lifted the bride's veil, she gasped. This was no princess, it was a dog! The minute the veil was lifted, the dog, who had been still and quiet till then, bit the old woman's nose. Before the rooster realised that he had been cheated, the dog jumped at him and killed him.

And that was the end of the old woman and her ambitions.

Walnut

'*d'u:n* - walnuts are tastiest when soaked in water for a few days before they are shelled and peeled to remove the skin

Three Childless Brothers and Their Children

There once were three brothers who lived together with their wives. Though their lives were comfortable, they were deeply unhappy because they had no children. One day as they were working in the garden, a holy man who was passing by saw them and approached the fence.

‘Why do all of you look so mournful? You have a beautiful home and garden, you are in good health, and it is a beautiful day. What troubles you so much that you cannot take pleasure in what you have?’ he asked.

The three brothers invited him indoors to rest. They offered him food and told him about the greatest sorrow of their lives—none of them had children.

The holy man listened in silence. After finishing his meal, he took three mangoes out of his canvas bag. ‘Eat these,’ he said, giving one to each brother, ‘and God will help you.’ Then, uttering a farewell blessing, he left.

The brothers ate the mangoes after dinner. Nine months later, each one’s wife gave birth to a healthy boy. The brothers’ lives overflowed with joy, and their home resounded with love and laughter. Their world was complete, and they lived blissfully in it, oblivious to everything outside. As time passed, the children grew, their bond as strong as that of brothers. Their fathers stayed in the happy bubble created by the birth of their children.

The fathers did not know that for some time now, a

dev had taken up residence in the city, spreading terror among the populace. People believed that he had come from across the sea.

One day, the cousins were practising their sword skills in the garden where their fathers had met the holy man years ago. The dev happened to be passing by and stopped to see the boys at their swordplay. Without any warning, he grabbed one of them and breathed on him. The boy turned into a little pebble which the dev put in his pocket. Seeing this, the other two ran home in fright and told their fathers what had happened.

The parents of the boy who had been turned into a pebble beat their heads and chests, they cried and howled and wailed, but none of this helped to bring their son back. They went to many powerful people in the city, requesting their help to fight the dev and restore their son to them. They pleaded in vain; the dev was so dreaded that nobody was willing to even consider helping the distraught parents.

Years passed. The two cousins, still children, grew stronger and more skilled. They still missed their cousin terribly, remembering clearly how the dev had turned him into a pebble and pocketed him. As they practised their moves one evening, they moved towards the jungle some distance away from their home. Unspoken, they shared the same thought: today would be the day they would find the dev, kill him and rescue their cousin.

As they went deeper into the jungle, they came upon a tall tree with an *agar pachhin's* nest perched right at the top with two little chicks in it. One of the cousins saw a serpent snaking its way towards the nest to make a meal of the chicks. He leapt up at the serpent, chopping it into pieces. In a short while, the mother agar pachhin returned and saw the cousins wielding their swords at the foot of the tree. Certain that they were trying to harm her fledglings, she prepared to attack and drive the boys away. As she was about to dive down, the chicks told her that these boys had killed a snake to protect them. Hearing this, she dived down to thank the boys for keeping her children safe. The three of them began talking and by the time the boys had to return home, she had become firm friends with them.

The boys reached home to find their uncle weeping

inconsolably yet again; the loss of his son was ever fresh, and he could not move on. The boys swore an oath that they would not rest until they had found the whereabouts of the dev who had stolen their cousin. They left the house immediately, and as they did so, they ran into the holy man who had given their fathers the mangoes, but the boys did not know this. The holy man asked them who they were and where they were headed. The boy who had cut up the snake said that they wanted to free their cousin from the clutches of the dev and asked for the holy man's blessing.

The holy man said, 'Son, the dev you seek lives across the seven seas, but this is not the time for you to go after him. Go back home. After all, you have fulfilled your vow. You now know the place where the dev can be found.'

The boys were unwilling to return but did not know how to negate the holy man's suggestion, so they bowed to him and turned their footsteps homeward.

Early the next morning, the boy who had saved the agar pachhin's children crept out of the house before dawn. He had spent the whole night awake, wondering whether or not to take his cousin with himself. Finally, he had decided it would be best for him to go alone. After all, who knew what fate had in store for him? If he were to come face to face with the dev and lose, at least one child would still be at home to solace the three sets of parents. He carried with him as much money and as many valuables as he could to help him succeed in his objective.

As he walked away from the house, he wondered how he would cross the seven seas to reach the place where the dev lived. He was still pondering this when a huge shadow seemed to descend on him. He looked up to find his friend, the agar pachhin, flying over him.

'Where are you going, my friend?' she asked.

The boy told her everything that had happened and said, 'I am on my way to kill the dev who lives across the seven seas.'

'Let me help you,' said the agar pachhin. 'Climb onto my back, hold on to my wings, and let me fly you across the seven seas.'

The boy climbed on, and she took off. When they landed, the agar pachhin said, 'This is where you'll find the dev.' She plucked a feather from her wing and gave it to him. 'If you ever need my help, hold this feather up to the sun, and I will come to you.'

The boy put the feather in his pocket and began looking for the dev. Wherever he looked, strange sights met his eyes. He saw people, but they were distorted, unlike any people he had ever seen before; he saw houses, but they were unlike any houses he had ever seen before; he saw *paris* and other beings he could not name. He walked on, constantly turning his head from left to right to take in every detail. His footsteps slowed when he reached what appeared to be a magnificent palace.

A strange force drew him in and he walked silently up to a door. When he opened it, he found himself looking into a grand room in which a *pari*-like woman appeared to be sleeping. She did not stir even when he walked into the room and gazed at her sleeping form. A large stone lay near the head of her bed and a necklace of beads lay at her feet. He picked up the necklace and put it around the woman's neck. She opened her eyes immediately and said, 'Boy, what are you doing here? The dev who has imprisoned me is about to arrive. If he finds you here, he will kill you. You are just a boy and cannot fight him.'

'I have come to kill a dev,' the boy replied. 'Tell me, where is the dev who has imprisoned you?'

'Don't be foolish, boy!' she said. 'Did you see the hundreds of stones in the courtyard as you came in? Each stone is actually a human being. He cast a spell on each one and turned them into stones. He kidnapped me years ago and now holds me captive in his palace.'

The boy was overjoyed. 'This is the very dev whom I have come to kill,' he said.

The pari could not believe her ears. 'Boy, you are still a child. You cannot kill him. Nobody can kill him.'

'Why not?'

'Because beyond this sea is yet another sea. Beyond that sea is a row of three shops. In the farthest shop is a parrot in a cage. The dev's life is contained within that parrot. As long as the parrot is alive, the dev cannot be killed.' She grew agitated. 'But go now! The dev may come back any moment and if he finds you here, he will either kill you or turn you into a stone.'

The boy left the palace, wondering how he would cross the sea and reach the parrot in the farthest shop. He remembered the feather the agar pachhin had given him and held it up to the sun. Almost instantly, the sky darkened with the shadow of the agar pachhin's enormous wingspan. She landed before him and said, 'You look worried. What is the matter? Why have you summoned me?'

The boy told her about his new problem. As before, she asked him to clamber onto her back, and flew him past the last sea to where he would find the row of shops. He dismounted and found himself in an even more unusual place than where the dev lived. There seemed to be endless rows of shops in every direction. How would he locate the shop that had the parrot? Firstly, it would take time, and secondly, the dev might find him and kill him before the parrot was found, which was certainly not part of the boy's plan. It was clear that if he could not find the parrot, the parrot would have to find him. He decided to use the money and valuables he had carried from home.

He walked the streets shouting loudly like a hawker selling his wares. But instead of asking people to buy something, the boy kept saying, 'Does anyone have a parrot for sale? I am a buyer of parrots.'

One shopkeeper stopped him and said, 'I have a parrot to sell, but it is very expensive.'

'How much?'

The merchant quoted an impossibly high price for the bird. The boy paid the amount without haggling, and the merchant handed over the caged parrot. The boy immediately reached through the bars of the cage and grabbed the parrot's neck in a tight grip.

The dev had reached home a short while after the boy had taken off on the agar pachhin's back. He sniffed hard and asked the pari, 'Tell me who came here in my absence.'

The pari did not want to anger the dev, but she also wanted to protect the boy so she said, 'Nobody.'

'You lie!' the dev thundered. 'I know that a human being has been here. I can smell it! Where have you hidden him? Tell me this instant!' He raised a fist and stepped towards her. It was at that very moment that across the vast sea, the boy grabbed the parrot's neck. The dev fell to the ground in the pari's room. Enraged, almost paralysed with pain, he screamed, 'Who came here in my absence? Who learnt about the parrot in which my life is preserved? Tell me!'

The pari just kept shaking her head.

In the meantime, the boy had summoned the agar

pachhin once more and was flying back to the dev's palace. He landed in the courtyard and walked up to the dev writhing in pain inside the pari's room, his hand still choking the neck of the caged parrot.

Gritting his teeth through agonising pain, the dev looked at the boy standing over him and said, 'Ask for anything you want, anything at all, but please let the parrot go. I will give you whatever you ask for, just release the bird.'

'I want you to reverse the spell you have cast. I want every stone in and around your courtyard to be turned back to what they were. Do it and I will free the parrot.'

The boy released his grip around the parrot's neck so that the dev could pick himself up from the floor. He staggered to the courtyard where hundreds of stones were strewn. The instant he reversed the spell, the previously empty courtyard was filled with hundreds of people. The boy located his cousin in the crowd and they embraced each other warmly. The boy then gave the parrot's neck a sharp twist, and the dev fell to the ground in agony. Another twist beheaded the bird, and the dev lay lifeless.

The pari ran out of the palace and thanked the

boy profusely for saving her. All those who had been restored to human form also expressed their heartfelt gratitude. As the people turned towards their homes, the boy lifted the feather the agar pachhin had given him. Almost instantly, she appeared with one of her children, ready to carry the cousins home, where the family rejoiced at being reunited.

Samovar

'səma:va:r - a copper kettle used to brew and serve tea, the central compartment has live coals while the ingredients for tea are put in the compartment around it, ensuring that after brewing, the tea stays hot for a long time

The Poor Man's Daughter

A poor man who had lost his wife had only one treasure in his life—his daughter, whom he loved dearly. As time passed, she reached the age of marriage but no suitors came forward to ask for her hand. The poor man waited patiently at first, but as months and years went by, he grew anxious. She had to be married off as soon as possible to the best match he could find, for how would she live after he was gone? And who would marry her if she was an old maid? These worries preyed on his mind day and night, and when he could find no solution, he decided to seek guidance from a sage.

The sage spent most of his time meditating under a tree on the outskirts of the village. The poor man waited for the sage to finish his meditation, and told him his problem. Without a word, the sage turned away to face the tree and leaned his forehead against the tree trunk. Both men sat in silence—the sage communing with the tree, and the poor man waiting for the sage's advice. When the sage finally turned to face the poor man, he said, 'Go home and rest easy tonight. In the morning, take your daughter's hand and step outside the house with her. Marry your daughter off to whoever you see first when you come outside, and she will have a happy married life. Remember, marry her to the very first one you meet.'

The poor man thanked the sage profusely and went home. For the first time in years, he slept soundly through the night. In the morning, he held his daughter's hand and stepped out of the house. The moment he did so, he saw a heavily built bear coming towards them. It seemed almost as if the bear had been waiting for them to come out. The bear was upon them before the poor man could run away or push his daughter to safety. It snatched the girl's hand from her father's grasp, held it firmly in its paw and lumbered away.

The girl kept screaming for her father but she was already too far away, and the poor man was too old and too slow and too weak to get her back from the bear. The man was heartbroken at being separated from his daughter in this way, and went back into the house feeling helpless. Despairing of ever meeting her again, he knew neither rest nor peace. Tears fell constantly from his eyes, tears he was often unaware of. When he had gathered his senses somewhat, he went back to the sage and lamented, 'What have you done, O holy one? My daughter is gone. Not only is she gone, she must be dead by now because the bear must have eaten her up. What have you done? Oh, what have you done? It would have been better for her to become an old maid.' His throat was raw from crying and his breath hitched in his throat.

The sage told him, 'Have faith and have patience. Go back home. Don't worry. See what happens.'

The poor man had no option but to return, weeping all the way. Through the night he wept, mourning his daughter. In the morning, when he opened his eyes, he thought that he must have lost his eyesight

or his mind, for standing in the doorway of the hut was his daughter, dressed like a queen. Next to her stood a handsome man whose clothes and bearing were that of a badshah. For some time, the poor man was too dumbstruck. He rubbed his eyes repeatedly, wondering if he was dreaming. But when his daughter came to embrace him, he finally believed that it was really her. He said, 'My daughter, what happened? Weren't you taken away by a fearsome bear?'

His daughter said, 'The bear was not really a bear. It was Raja Indra who, disguised as a bear, had come from *patal* to take me away.'

The newlyweds spent some time with the poor man and after they left, he went to tell the sage what had happened.

The sage smiled and said, 'Faith is the secret. If you put your trust in God, you will always achieve your goal. Even if you feel you are all alone and there is no one to support you, even if you feel everyone has abandoned you, do not abandon your faith. Because God will not abandon you and will not let you suffer.'

The poor man folded his hands in reverence and went home smiling.

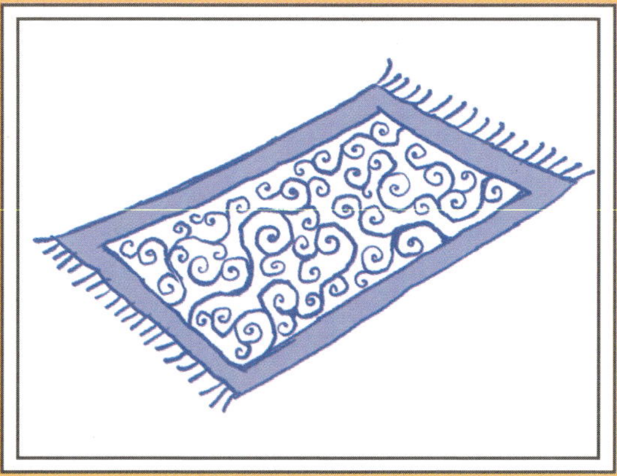

Carpet

ˈkəɪliːn - the rich have carpets of wool and silk, while the poor use mats of straw

The Bald Man and the Rantas

An elderly woman had a young son who was bald. He was both witty and cunning, like all bald characters in Kashmiri folktales. One day, he told his mother, 'Look, Ma, I found an apricot seed! What should I do with it?'

'Plant it in the courtyard,' said his mother.

When he had planted the seed, he said, 'O Seed, if by tomorrow you have not become a seedling, I will dig you out of the earth and throw you on the rubbish heap.'

Early the next morning, the bald man rushed to the courtyard. A small apricot seedling grew where he had planted the seed. He was thrilled at the sight and said, 'Hey Seedling, if by tomorrow you haven't transformed into a full-grown apricot tree, I will uproot you and throw you away.'

The next morning, the man saw a large apricot tree where the seedling had been. 'Tree, listen well! If by tomorrow you are not laden with apricots, I will cut you down and uproot your stump.'

The next morning, the bald man found the tree laden with ripe apricots. He climbed the tree and began eating its delicious fruit. As he was eating apricots high up in the tree, he saw a woman coming towards the house. She looked like she was his *khala*. The woman stopped under the tree and said, 'O bald one, my son, please give me some apricots. They look so delicious.

I am your khala, so you should share them with me.'

The man looked down and saw that it was indeed his aunt. 'Of course I'll give you the apricots, khala *jaan*,' he said. 'I'll just throw them down and you can have them.'

The woman said, 'No, my son. Why don't you come down? If you throw the fruit from such a height, it will get squashed. Come down and hand me the fruit.'

The bald man agreed. What he did not know was that the woman was not his khala but a rantas. Just as he handed her the apricots, she grabbed him and put him in a sack. Then she tied the mouth of the sack and carried him away to her house, which was at a great distance. After walking for a few hours, she was tired and hungry. When she saw a farmer ploughing his land, she put the sack down and said, '*Bhaisahab*, can you keep an eye on my sack? I want to go freshen up and get myself some food.'

The farmer agreed.

The bald man waited quietly inside the sack for the rantas to be out of hearing range and began shouting, 'Is there anyone here who can free me from this sack?' He kept hollering for a while.

The farmer heard the sound and came to investigate. As he got closer, he heard what the voice was saying and rushed to open the sack. He was shocked when he saw the bald man stuffed inside the sack. The farmer helped him out. They decided to trick the rantas so they filled the sack with mud, tying its mouth securely.

When the rantas returned, she saw the sack lying just as she had left it. Hefting it over her shoulders, she made her way home. On the way, she felt that the man was digging his knees into her back and she shouted, 'Bald one, I know you are trying to make it harder for me to carry you. Let me get home and I'll teach you a lesson you'll never forget. Wait and see what I do to you.'

Once home, she set the sack down in her courtyard and called for her daughter. 'I have caught a human being today,' she said. 'Once we've cooked him, we will feast on him.' She went indoors to rest, leaving her daughter to deal with the bald man.

When the daughter opened the sack, she hollered for her mother. The rantas, who had not even had a chance to sit down, came rushing and saw that the sack was filled with mud. Furious at being cheated, she resolved to catch the bald man in time for the next day's dinner. In the morning, the rantas, disguised as the bald man's *phuphi* this time, went to the apricot-laden tree and found him greedily gobbling fruit off the branches.

'Son, O bald one!' she called, 'Won't you give me some of the apricots?'

'Phuphi!' the bald man responded, 'Of course I will. Let me throw some down to you.'

'That's very rude. I don't want to eat fruit off the ground. I'm hungry and there's nowhere to wash the apricots,' she said. 'Why don't you come down and give them to me?'

Just the previous day, the bald man had been captured by a rantas who had come disguised as his aunt. Now he was facing yet another aunt who was saying the same things the rantas had said the previous day, but he was so focussed on eating the apricots that he did not pay attention. He just wanted to get rid of the interruption and climb to the higher branches to stuff himself with even more fruit. So he scrambled down, his hands and pockets overflowing with apricots.

The rantas, instead of reaching for the fruit, clamped a hand on his arm and again stuffed him into a sack. This time she did not make the mistake of stopping on the way. She soldiered on till she got home. 'I've caught the man today,' she told her daughter when she reached home, and went inside to rest.

When the girl opened the sack and saw the bald man, she fell in love with him. What could she do now? Her mother was expecting her to chop up the man and add him to the cooking pot! Taking a deep breath, she told her mother, 'Why don't we wait till the evening before we cook him?'

The rantas said, 'That's a good idea. I'm really tired from carrying him all that distance. I'll enjoy the hot meal more when I'm somewhat rested.' In a short while, she fell asleep, her mouth slightly open, her snores echoing throughout the house.

All the strength, power and magic of a rantas is in her hair, and the only way to strip away her power is to tie up her hair, which her daughter obviously knew. When she saw that the rantas was sound asleep, she tied her mother's hair to a stake. Then she rushed to the man and said, 'Bald Sir, I have fallen in love with you. I wish to marry you.'

He said, 'Your mother is preparing to eat me and you say you want to marry me! Your mother will beat you before she eats me.'

The girl said, 'No, I have tied her hair to a stake. You see, the power of a rantas is in her hair, and if you tie it up, all her strength drains away, and she is feebler than a newborn kitten.'

The man's eyes began to sparkle. He said, 'Yes, I will marry you, but wait for a day. My body is cramped and aching from being stuffed inside a sack.'

The bald man and the rantas's daughter sat together and talked for a while. She showed him everything in the house, including the gold, silver and precious stones that she and her mother had amassed. Then he said, 'You look tired. Lie down and let me massage your legs. You'll be rested and relaxed for the wedding tomorrow.'

The rantas's daughter agreed, and enjoyed the massage. When she was so relaxed that she fell asleep, the bald man tied her hair to a stake, packed all the valuables in the house into a bundle and set off for his home.

Pheran

'pherən - a long loose woollen coat worn as the outermost layer of clothing

The Man Who Wanted to Be Rich

There was once a man who lived happily with his wife. They did not have much money, but they managed with whatever he earned. Soon, they were expecting their first baby. The man was worried about how they would feed an extra mouth. So he worked harder and his income increased. Since there were three of them now, his increased income did not make them any richer but they did not become any poorer either.

In a year's time, they were expecting a second baby, and the man wondered how much poorer they would become as a result of this second child. But once again, his income increased just enough to offset the extra expenses on account of the second child.

In this way, the couple had seven daughters in ten years. By now, the man was earning quite well but everything he brought home was spent in feeding and clothing the family of nine. One night, he was not able to sleep. 'I earn so well,' he thought, 'if only I did not have children, then my wife and I could be rich.' He had worked hard all his life and he was not looking forward to working hard for as long as he lived. He wanted to enjoy a luxurious life with his wife while they were still young and energetic enough to do so.

Once the thought had entered his head, it would not leave. Every waking moment that he was not occupied with something else, he wondered how his life would be if he were rich.

One day he decided to do something about it. Telling his wife that he was taking the children to a fair in town, he set off with them. They crossed meadows and rivers and were walking through a jungle when they came across a stream. They were all tired, especially the younger girls, and the man said they would stop there for a while.

'Take care of your sisters. I'm going upstream to see if I can find some food for all of you,' he said to his eldest daughter. To the other girls he said, 'Drink some water and freshen up. Listen to your eldest sister and wait here till I return,' and walked deeper into the jungle.

He walked for a short distance to ensure he was out of earshot and out of sight in case any of the girls decided to look for him, and hid behind a thick copse of trees until the sun began to set. Tearing off a bit of his pheran, he dropped it into the stream and slowly released into the water some red powder from a box that he carried. He wanted his children to see the fragment of pheran and the red-coloured water in the stream and think that a bear must have killed their father.

Feeling very pleased with himself at having accomplished his objective, he made his way home. His wife, who was preparing the evening meal, was

startled to see him walk into the house alone, with stooped shoulders and tears in his eyes. Frantic, she asked him where the children were. He told her that the boat they had taken to cross the river had capsized, and all the children had drowned and been carried away by the current. He told her that he had almost not had the courage to come home to her, but had finally returned to tell her what had happened. The woman wept and wailed, inconsolable at having lost all her children in this cruel way. The man pretended to share her heartbreak, but in his heart of hearts, he was looking forward to saving a lot of money and finally living a life of greater ease.

But when he went to work, he found that he could only earn enough to feed his wife and himself. If the children had been with him, they would have starved. He worked ever harder but still only earned enough to support himself and his wife.

After a week, the man realised how blinded he had been by his ego and greed. It was not his hard work that had brought in the money. It was God who had always made sure that he had enough to feed his family. Now that his family was reduced to just himself and his wife, he continued to make enough to feed the two of them—no more, no less.

The man was filled with remorse and shame that he had betrayed his children, that he had abandoned them on purpose. Hoping against hope, looking for redemption, he ran to the place where he had left his children. But it had been more than a week since he had left them. Obviously, there was no one there. He wondered if they had found shelter and food. He wondered if they were still together. He wondered if they were safe, if they were alive. He ran in all directions, calling out their names, tearing at his hair and his clothes but no answering voice came to his ears.

The trees stood silent, the sun moved slowly across the sky, the stream gurgled on. They knew but they were not telling. His heart in pieces, he put one foot in front of the other to return home.

Apples

ts'uːŋth - red, golden and green apples grow and are eaten, the latter often cooked as a vegetable with potatoes or brinjals

The Foolish King

A group of wandering *fakirs* arrived at a kingdom one morning. It was the most beautiful kingdom they had ever seen. As they approached its borders, they could see terraced farms of rice and sesame ready to be harvested. They saw gurgling streams, with lush grass and wildflowers on either side, as they walked along the broad road. Dappled sunlight shone through the leaves of the large walnut trees lining the road. Their steps quickened in anticipation as they approached the city.

The city was clean, with well-maintained houses and roads, and everyone they saw was well-dressed. As the fakirs went around the city begging for alms, they noticed something they'd never seen before. Everything in the markets was sold at the same price. A kilo of rice cost the same as a kilo of coal, which cost the same as a kilo of gold.

The next morning, as the group prepared to leave the city, one of the fakirs approached the leader of the group. 'I think this is a great place,' he said. 'We can eat well for very little money, and it's so clean and pretty. Why don't we stay here for a few days?'

'No,' said the leader. 'Things are not created equal, you know. If everything here is available at the same price, this must be a dangerous place. If something goes wrong, we cannot be sure that justice will be meted out. I think we should leave immediately.'

'I think I'll stay on, if it's alright with you,' the fakir said.

No matter how hard the leader and the others tried, they could not convince the fakir to accompany them as they left the city. 'If you are in trouble, send me a message,' said the leader, telling the fakir where the group was headed.

The next morning, the city was buzzing with the news of a large theft. When the king was told about it, he asked his soldiers to round up all the strangers in the city and bring them to court. The fakir was the only stranger in the city and he was presented to the king with his arms tied behind his back.

'My kingdom has had no thefts for many months, and there's a robbery the day you enter it. It stands to reason that you are the criminal,' declared the king.

The fakir protested that he had not committed the theft, then he swore it, but the king was not interested in his assurances. The more vehemently the fakir protested, the more annoyed the king became.

'First you steal, then you protest when you are accused of the crime, and now you have the audacity to insist upon your innocence! I will make such an example of you that no stranger will ever dare even to think of committing a crime in my kingdom,' thundered the king. 'Put him in prison and hang him in the public square tomorrow!' he ordered.

The soldiers took the fakir away and threw him into prison.

Tears rolled down the fakir's face as he banged his head against the prison walls in despair. If only he had listened to the wise words of the old fakir, the leader of their group! But no amount of regret or crying over his fate would save him. Eventually, he sat with his head in his hands, too numb even to think.

Towards the evening, the prison guard came to him and said, 'Today is the last day of your life because you will be hanged in the morning. Do you want to meet someone, your family or a friend, before you die? We will have to send word to them today.'

The fakir remembered the old fakir's words. He told the guard where the group of fakirs would be found and requested him to send them a message. He remained awake all night, alternating between worrying and praying, hoping that the leader of the fakirs would come in time and find some way to save him from being hanged.

In the morning, the fakir was dragged to the public square, where the gallows had already been set up. The city wore an air of festivity, and the square was crowded with people wanting to see the 'thief' hanged. The noose was prepared, and beside it stood the masked hangman, ready to carry out his grim task. All was in readiness, awaiting the king's arrival. As the fakir was brought to the stairs leading to the gallows, the leader of the group of fakirs approached him. The guard was about to push him aside when the fakir said, 'He is the man I sent a message to!'

The guard nodded and stood aside, saying, 'You can speak to him for a couple of minutes, but you'll have to stop the minute the king gets here.'

The leader of the fakirs leaned towards the condemned fakir's ear and whispered, 'When the king arrives, I will beg him to hang me instead of you. Each time I do this, you must protest forcefully and say, "No, Badshah sahab, don't allow him to be hanged. Please hang me." Each time I ask the king to hang me, you need to say this strongly enough to convince him that you want to be hanged. Leave the rest to me.'

Before the fakir could wonder how this stratagem would save him, a fanfare of trumpets announced that the sovereign had arrived. As the king ascended the throne, the leader of the fakirs prostrated himself at the monarch's feet. He said, 'Badshah sahab, please be merciful towards this fellow. He is the only son of a sick woman. If he is put to death, who will look after her in her old age? I am old and don't have much longer to live. Also, I have no dependants. Please hang me instead of him, Badshah sahab! It will be a kindness.'

The condemned fakir shouted, 'No! No, Badshah sahab! You condemned me to death, so I am the one who should be hanged! It would be unjust of you to hang him! Hang me! Please, hang me!'

The leader of the fakirs interrupted again and again, each time giving the king different reasons why he should be the one hanged instead of the fakir who was in chains. And each time, the fakir followed his leader's advice and protested vociferously, saying that since he was the one who had been condemned, he should be the one put to death.

Each time, the king looked in disbelief from one to the other as each asked that he be put to death. When this had gone on for a while, the king grew increasingly curious. Both men were eager to die. Could there be a reason for this? He asked both fakirs to approach him and ordered his courtiers to step away. Quietly, the king asked, 'What is all this? All my life I have seen people arguing and fighting for their lives to be spared.

But today, both of you are eager to be hanged. Tell me, what is the reason for your strange behaviour?'

The old fakir said, 'Badshah sahab, if you get your priests to read you the Book of Saints, you will find that today is the most auspicious day to die. The person who dies today will definitely go to paradise, even if he is the greatest sinner who ever lived. But this secret is known only to a chosen few.'

The king had been foolish all his life. As he grew older, he was increasingly troubled by the realisation that he had been greedy throughout his life. His greed for power, wealth and the throne had led him to commit many evil deeds. But now, as he was in the second half of his life, his main focus was on how to avoid going to hell in the afterlife. In fact, for the past few years, most of his time had been spent in making priests conduct numerous rituals which would guarantee him a place in heaven after his death—a place that even he knew he did not deserve. When he heard the old fakir's words, the king saw a golden opportunity to reach his goal.

He gestured to the fakirs to be quiet and step aside. When he stood up and raised his arms, the crowd which had been clamouring to see the hanging fell silent.

'My dear people!' the king announced, 'according to the holy books, today is the most auspicious day to die. Anyone who dies today is assured a place in heaven. Knowing this, I would like to give up my life today.'

There was a hush all around at this announcement.

'Guards! I order you to release this man and to hang me instead so that my soul may go to heaven,' the king ordered.

A chorus of protests arose at the king's order, but he was, after all, the king, and so his orders had to be obeyed, no matter how foolish they were. The noose and the hangman were ready. All that remained was for the guards to march the king onto the platform and put his head in the noose. As this happened, the crowd watched with renewed enthusiasm. As for the fakirs, the minute the king finished his announcement, they elbowed their way through the crowd and took to their heels as soon as they found the path clear, thanking their lucky stars at their escape.

Kehwa tea leaves

'kehvə - a green tea made with cinnamon, cardamom, cloves, and saffron which is usually sweetened and garnished with crushed almonds

Shal Jamadari

(The Jackals' Association)

In a jungle lived a lion who hunted and ate one jackal every single day. While the jackals understood that the lion had to eat so he could live, they found it unfair that he had given up hunting all other animals except for them. The jackals decided to get together to discuss how to tackle this problem. Their first step was to create an association to encourage every single jackal to participate. Each of them signed up enthusiastically. Naturally, the first matter under consideration was how to be rid of the menace of the lion hunting them, and only them, every single day.

On the appointed day and at the designated time, they gathered in a forest clearing early in the morning. The lion had eaten just the previous evening, so they knew they were safe from him till the evening. Many jackals spoke, sharing the physical, mental and emotional stress they were undergoing because of the lion. Then they turned their minds to figuring out a solution—some wondered if there was some way to drive the lion out of this part of the jungle, while others suggested that they try to reason with him that he should hunt other animals as well. Though there was a lot of talk, they were not convinced that any one way was better than the others. Finally, some jackals said they should seek the oldest jackal's advice. He was physically weak, which is why he had not joined the meeting, but was known for his cunning. He also had a lot of experience because he was significantly older than any of the other jackals. He came out of his den just once a day, to eat.

A small group of jackals went to speak to him, asking how they could solve their problem. The old jackal said, 'I am old now. I hardly ever leave my den. What can I do? What do you expect from me?'

The other jackals said, 'We seek your invaluable advice drawn from your vast experience. Our *jamadari* is incomplete without your presence. You must join us and give us your guidance.'

The old jackal refused many times, but they would not take no for an answer. Finally, walking out of his den, he said, 'Since you all insist, I will join your meeting.' When the pack reached the forest clearing, they made the old jackal sit on a ledge on top of a mound so all of them could look at him when he spoke. He drew a deep breath and said, 'Jackal brothers! There are so many of us that if we were to hunt down the lion, each of us would get only one morsel of meat. We can get together and attack him, kill him and remove him from this earth.'

This was a startling idea to all of them. Attack a lion? But as they thought about it, they felt it was the best way to resolve the issue. The clearing was soon filled with shouts of 'Yes!', 'That's what we'll do!' and 'Great idea!'

The oldest jackal said, 'Can all of you fight the lion?'

In one voice, they responded, 'Yes!'

The oldest jackal raised his voice and asked once more, 'Can all of you fight the lion?'

They responded, 'Yes!'

The oldest jackal asked the question yet again. The third time, the other jackals' positive response was deafening.

The oldest jackal continued, 'Then we need a leader who will plan the attack and give the order so that everyone does what they are supposed to do at the time they are supposed to do it. If we all attack randomly, we will be uncoordinated and the lion will defeat us easily.'

The jackals agreed and said, 'There is no better leader than you. We have decided to appoint you as our leader. You are the best person for the job.'

The oldest jackal protested, 'Brothers, I am old and weak. I cannot do anything. Choose someone else as your leader.'

But the jackals were determined. When they assured him repeatedly that he was the only one capable of leading them, his ego, which had been dampened by his age and weakness, stirred. He had believed himself to be old, weak and retired, but they were right. He could still be their leader. They were keen to follow him, and what did he have to do, after all? Just give them orders, which they would obey. He gave in with good grace. 'Alright brothers, as you wish. I will be your leader. Here's what we'll do. This place where I am now sitting will be my seat. It is on high ground, and I am able to see all around for quite a distance. When the lion comes, I will see him and warn all of you to get ready. And when I give the order, you can attack as a pack.'

There was an excited chorus of agreement from the jackals. Then one of them said, 'But if we are all moving around, how will we know who our leader is? It is not easy to identify one of us, and definitely not when we are in the middle of a fight. There should be some way for us to identify our leader easily.'

The oldest jackal said, 'Look for a token which will identify the leader.'

One of the jackals found a rough leather patch which they tied to the top of the oldest jackal's tail. The patch was wider than the jackal's girth so that it was clearly visible from a distance. It was so large that the lower part of it dragged on the ground when the jackal walked or moved his tail, and when it dragged, it made a loud sound. Now they would all be able to recognise their leader by both sight and sound.

All was in readiness. The jackals waited for their leader to see the lion, and for his command to attack it.

As evening fell, the lion came roaring out of his lair. The sound frightened half the life out of every jackal there. When the lion roared a second time, every jackal had only one thought: to flee. When the lion roared a third time, there wasn't a single jackal left in the clearing; they had hidden in the closest den they could find. Even their leader, the oldest jackal, rose on shaky legs and staggered away to find shelter in a den.

But as he straggled in, the leather patch got stuck in the doorway of the den and the jackal couldn't enter it fully. The jackals who were already hidden deep inside encouraged him, saying, 'Come in, Sir. Come in quickly and be safe.'

The old jackal yelled in desperation, 'Can someone take this leadership from me? Just take it from me, remove it! My leadership token is stuck–I want to be rid of it!'

The lion, not finding a single jackal in the forest, followed the noise, and saw the oldest jackal stuck at the mouth

of a den. He caught the leather patch in his jaws and dragged the oldest jackal out. One swipe of his paw, and the old jackal lay flat on the ground. The lion held his prey in his mouth and trotted away to eat it at leisure.

After the lion had left, the jackals emerged from their dens, shook their heads and said, 'It was leadership that caused the death of the old jackal.'

This story explains the Kashmiri phrase *shal jamadari*: Whenever the leader of an organisation faces a difficult situation, it is called shal jamadari.

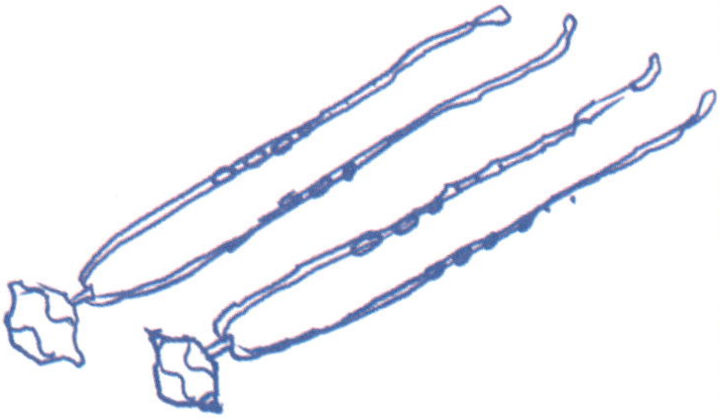

Dejhor

'dejhəʊr - earrings a girl wears at the time of her marriage for as long as her husband is alive; the long gold chain goes through a hole in the cartilage of her ear and is given by the groom's family, while the pendant at the end of the chain is given by her family

The Two Princes

A king and his queen would climb to the top of their palace every evening to sit and look at their kingdom. One evening when they got to the roof, they found that a pair of birds had built a nest in a watchtower. A few days later, two chicks were born in the nest. The royal couple saw the parents constantly bringing grain and worms to feed their chicks.

This pattern was rudely interrupted. One evening, the king and queen arrived to see the female bird fallen on the stone roof. The chicks were cheeping piteously, while the male turned his motionless mate this way and that, prodding her with his beak but to no avail. Clearly, she was dead.

The next day, there was another female bird in the nest. She was feeding the chicks but when the queen looked closely, she saw that the bird was feeding them thorns, not grains or seeds or worms or fruit. The following evening, the queen found the two chicks dead. The queen thought that thorns must have got stuck in their throats and they must have choked to death. This affected the queen so strongly that she stopped going to the roof with the king in the evenings, discontinued her royal duties, and even stopped eating and drinking.

For a few days, the king let her be, but when she remained sorrowful and didn't reveal the cause of her distress, he decided to ask her what had upset her so deeply.

She said, 'One thought preys on my mind. We have two sons, the younger one just a toddler. If I die, promise me that you will not remarry. Our sons will not have a stepmother.'

The king realised that she was fixated on this idea and thought that the only way to help her recover was to swear an oath. 'You are healthy and young. There is nothing wrong with you, and nothing will happen to you. But if it gives you peace, I promise that I will make sure our sons do not have a stepmother,' he promised.

The queen recovered and things went back to normal. Days, then weeks, then months, then a few years passed. The princes grew up, but they were still young boys. The queen contracted a mysterious illness. Numerous *hakims* examined her, every cure and nostrum was tried, but to no avail.

On her deathbed, the queen summoned her sons and told them to visit her chestnut mare every day in the stable. She was the only chestnut mare in the entire kingdom and had been with the queen since she was a young girl. The queen's family had presented the mare as a wedding gift, knowing she could not bear to be separated from the horse for even a day. The queen said, 'She will miss me terribly, because I will not be around to ride her around the kingdom. Right now, you are too young to ride her. But if you visit the stables every evening, you can pat her and caress her and she won't miss me quite as much as she otherwise would. When you grow up, you can ride her.' The princes promised to look after the chestnut mare. Later that evening, the queen passed away.

The motherless princes kept their word and visited the stables every day to spend time with their mother's chestnut mare. The king also remained true to his promise and did not remarry.

This was the source of both hope and despair for one witch. This witch wanted her sister to be the queen of the kingdom. So long as the king did not marry anyone else, she could use her magic to make him marry her sister. But the king was determined to keep his promise to his late wife and refused every offer of marriage that came his way. So how would she make him marry her sister?

The witch needed help, and she knew just the person to turn to. She was friends with one of the serving maids in the palace. She would have to get the serving maid to help her. Using a mix of bribery, cajolery and threats, she convinced the maid to assist her. The maid in her turn approached a greedy minister in the king's cabinet, luring him with the promises of great riches and threatening him with the witch's magic. Together, the maid and minister conspired to get the king to marry the witch's sister.

The minister approached the king and said, 'You are the king, the supreme leader of this kingdom. It is not appropriate for you to make promises to women and spend your entire life enslaved to those promises. You are the king. You need a partner who will support you and work with you to govern the land. A queen has so many duties, and someone needs to fulfil them. Think of the kingdom. *You* may not need a companion, but the kingdom needs a queen.'

The king walked out of the chamber in anger. But over time, little by little, the minister wore down the king's objections, until at last, the king agreed to wed. The first thing the king did when his new wife arrived at the palace was to tell her about the promise he had made to his late wife. '*You* are my wife now. Please be kind to my sons. Be a good mother to them.'

The witch's sister said, 'You need not worry. They are my children now, and I will look after them accordingly.'

In the next few years, she gave birth to her own children, but as they grew up, the new queen grew increasingly worried. The late queen's sons were the first heirs to the throne, so it was natural that they would inherit the kingdom, not her own children. This thought was like a thorn in her side. Finally, she could not tolerate it any longer and told her sister, the witch, about it.

The witch cackled and handed her sister a small bottle. 'Here is a poison. Just add it to your stepsons' dinner. The effect of this poison will not be outwardly visible, and no physician, no matter how skilled, will be able to identify the poison or even to perceive that the boys have been poisoned. You'll be rid of the boys with no trouble at all.'

The queen hid the bottle in her clothing and returned to the palace with a much lighter heart.

That evening, as usual, the princes visited the chestnut mare in the stables. As they patted her, they noticed that tears were flowing from her eyes. They lay their heads against her flanks, fondled her ears and petted her on the forehead. All of a sudden, she began to speak. 'Both of you will be poisoned at dinner today. If you refuse to eat, you will be force-fed. To save yourselves, you must go to the attic after dinner. There you will find a rope made of hairs from my tail. Rub the rope vigorously all over your body, and the poison won't affect you.'

As soon as the princes began eating dinner, it felt like some force had taken over their insides. Though they felt terribly unwell, they neither had a fever nor did they feel any pain. They didn't vomit or lose consciousness. Excusing themselves as soon as they could after the meal, they rushed to the attic, where each brother rubbed the other hard with the rope made of horsehair.

In the morning, when the queen woke up, she found that the princes were still alive. As soon as she could, she rushed to the witch to inform her that the poison had not worked.

The witch used her magic powers and found out what had happened. 'It is their mother's mare in the stable who has been advising them. That is why they still live. But you won't have to worry about the mare for very long,' she said. 'When you get home, take to your bed and pretend to be ill. I will arrange with a hakim to prescribe the liver of a chestnut mare as the only cure. Since this is the only chestnut mare in the kingdom, that will put an end to the mare, and then we can proceed with our plans for the princes.'

The witch found an unscrupulous hakim who was willing to do the deed for a bag of gold. He had no idea that the princes were the witch's real target. If the queen wanted the chestnut mare dead and chose this roundabout method to achieve the result, so be it. Things proceeded according to plan. When the hakim told the king that only the liver of a chestnut mare could cure the queen, he consulted his ministers.

'What is the problem, Badshah sahab? There is a chestnut mare in the royal stables, and she is old. Let us feed her liver to the queen,' his most trusted advisor said.

The king knew how much the late queen had treasured the chestnut mare, but he realised that he could not lose his queen for a horse. Reluctantly, he ordered that the chestnut mare be slaughtered. The princes raised an outcry, protesting the decision. The mare was the only memento they had of their mother, and they wanted to ensure she lived a long and happy life.

But the king lost his temper with them. 'The queen is also your mother, isn't she? How can it be that having already lost one mother, you are prepared to lose another one as well? I will not listen to one more word of protest. The mare will definitely be slaughtered.'

The heartbroken princes rushed to the stable, and crying bitterly, told the mare about the king's decision. She was calm. 'Here is what we will do,' she said. 'Tell the king that you would like to ride me one last time before I am killed. That is all you have to do. I will take care of the rest.'

The princes returned to the palace and requested the king to grant them one last ride on the chestnut mare before she was killed. The king, happy to see their calm acceptance of his decision, was pleased to grant their wish.

The next morning, the chestnut mare was brought out of her stable and taken to a large stadium where numerous sporting events were held. The audience stands were full; people had come to watch the only chestnut mare in the kingdom being ridden by the princes before she was taken to be killed. The king announced, 'Let the princes have their wish. Let them take three rounds of this field on the chestnut mare.' Then a thought struck him, and he added, 'If the mare tries to escape, the person over whom she jumps will be beheaded.' Hearing this, everyone in the audience stood up to make it harder for the mare to escape.

The princes swung up into the saddle, and the mare began cantering. She completed two rounds and accelerated to a gallop in the third round. Halfway through the final round, she veered off course, jumped over the head of the king and vanished from sight. A contingent of soldiers drew their swords and mounted their horses to give chase, for not only had the mare disappeared, she had also taken the princes with herself. The soldiers followed the mare's tracks, but there was no sign of her. They rode till they were deep in the jungles. Finally, acknowledging defeat, they returned to the palace.

Let us leave the king and queen here and see what happened to the princes.

The mare rode far, crossing many forests and streams, carrying the princes ever farther from their home, the kingdom where the queen wanted to kill them. When she finally stopped, the princes dismounted and sat in the shade of a chinar. Asking the two princes to find food for themselves, the mare walked to a green patch a short distance away and began to nibble grass. The princes, too tired to move, continued to rest under the tree. After some time, the mare returned and said, 'This is where we have to go our separate ways. But here is one hair from my tail. If you should ever need me, hold this hair up to the sun, and I will be in front of you.' The mare trotted away and was soon lost to sight.

Fear of their fate and that of the chestnut mare's, coupled with the desperate ride away from the kingdom had exhausted both princes. Only sleep would restore their energies, but how could they sleep securely in an unknown forest with nobody to watch over them? The elder prince decided to sleep first while his brother kept watch.

The younger prince walked to and fro to avoid falling asleep. As he was pacing, he saw two birds alight on the branch of a tree and begin chirping to each other. He was amazed that he could understand what they said.

One bird said, 'Budabror, look at those birds sitting on the branch of that tree near the spring.'

The younger prince turned his head towards the spring and saw two songbirds sitting on a branch.

'Do you know what kind of birds they are?' the bird continued.

Budabror replied, 'Sudabror, they are magical birds. It is said that whoever eats the flesh of one will become a king, while the person who eats the flesh of the other bird will become a minister.'

When the younger prince heard this, he got very excited. Not only would he find food for himself and his brother, but they would also become king and minister! The only problem was how to catch and kill the birds before they flew away. Since they were supposed to be riding the chestnut mare around the field, neither of the princes had any weapons with themselves. The prince walked around quietly, keeping one eye on the songbirds, as he looked for something that would be a suitable weapon. After some time, he found the broken branch of a tree on the forest floor. The branch ended in a point that he hoped would be sharp enough to kill the songbirds. He picked it up, aimed it and let it go. Straight as an arrow it flew, piercing both birds at the same time. He built a small fire and cooked the birds, eating one and leaving the other for his brother.

The elder prince ate the other bird as soon as he awoke and told his brother, 'Stay here. I will look for a settlement and ask the people for shelter.' He held out the hair from the horse's tail and continued, 'Take this and keep it safely. If you face any problem, hold this hair up to the sun and summon the chestnut mare. She will help you. Be alert and wait. I will be back soon.'

The younger prince took the hair, nodded his head at everything his elder brother told him and promised to stay there and wait.

Waving goodbye, the elder prince set off. He walked for many hours but did not find any sign of human habitation. It was late in the afternoon when he saw a man walking towards him from what seemed to be a village. He asked the man, 'Will I be able to find something to eat in that place?'

The man said, 'There is a *harissawala* who will give you some *harissa*.'

The prince walked on, asking villagers he met for directions to the harissawala. When he reached, he found himself in a spacious courtyard where a man and a girl were sitting. He asked the harissawala for food, and the man asked the prince to sit on the *chatai* laid out in one corner of the courtyard. The prince had no idea that the harissawala had dug a large, deep hole in the courtyard and had covered it with a chatai. Whenever strangers or travellers came looking for food, he asked them to sit on the chatai. They would fall into the hole, and late at night, he would kill them and make harissa from their flesh.

The girl's eyes followed every step the prince took as he walked across the courtyard to the chatai. She had never seen such a handsome young man with such a regal bearing. One look, and she had fallen in love with him. She was determined to save him from her father.

As one would expect, the minute the prince sat on the chatai, he fell into the pit. When the sun set, the harissawala's daughter led the prince out of the pit and locked him in a dilapidated storage room in an outhouse. She told her father that when she went to get the prince out of the pit, he had overpowered her and escaped. Every day, she took him food in secret and spent as much time with him as she dared.

In this way, twelve years passed.

But what had happened to the younger prince?

When his elder brother did not come back even though most of the day had passed, the younger prince wondered if he should hold the horse's hair up to the sun. But just then, he saw a group of people passing by, talking cheerfully amongst themselves. A man from the group called out, 'Are you lost? You are too young to be here all by yourself. Come with us.'

The younger prince was used to doing what people asked him to do, since he was usually the youngest of everyone present, so he joined the group. Unfortunately, the group went in the opposite direction to the one the elder prince had taken. They walked for a while till at last they reached what appeared to be a city. There was a great hustle and bustle, *dhols* were being beaten, and people were dressed in their best and were moving with purpose. The group with the young prince joined the crowds. As they walked, he overheard people saying that since the king of this city had died without an heir, a new ruler was to be chosen. They halted in a large square. On a raised platform in the middle of the square, drummers wielded their sticks with renewed vigour before falling silent.

A man on the platform addressed the crowd. 'We are gathered here to choose a new ruler. According to custom, the elephant will soon be released, as will the hawk. The person the elephant bows to and the one on whom the hawk lands will be chosen as the king of the land. This custom has given us many great kings, and we are sure it will not fail us now. Now that everyone who wishes to be considered for the position is here, let the elephant and the hawk be released.'

In a few minutes, the hawk circled in the sky above the crowd and the elephant could be seen at one end of the square. People made way for the elephant as it walked slowly through the crowd. It stopped when it came in front of the younger prince and bent its knees.

There was the sudden flap of wings—the hawk landed on his shoulder. There was a moment of complete silence, then the entire square erupted in cheers. Dhols were beaten and trumpets were blown to signal that the new king had been chosen.

The younger prince was trained in all the skills of statecraft and became proficient in them after a few years. He was so immersed in his training and his new life that after some time, he forgot that he had ever had a brother. He was a just ruler and administered the kingdom well.

One day, after twelve years had passed, the younger prince, now the ruler, suddenly remembered his elder brother and all the events that had led to their separation. His grief and regret were boundless: how could he have forgotten his brother, who had been an inseparable part of his life till they were separated? He thought back to the chestnut mare's hair he had taken from his brother. He must have lost it while walking towards the city with the group. At any rate, he definitely could not locate the hair now, after all this time. And the chestnut mare had already been old when he was a little boy. Would she even be alive now?

But he was sure of one thing: no matter what, he had to locate his brother.

He could not forgive himself for having forgotten his brother and immediately issued a proclamation throughout the kingdom asking people to come forward and tell him a brother's story. Drummers and announcers went from village to village and town to town, repeating the king's proclamation throughout the kingdom. Eventually, they reached the village where the elder prince had been kept in hiding by the harissawala's daughter.

The elder prince heard the noise and asked the girl what the excitement was about. She told him that the king of the land had issued a proclamation asking to hear a brother's story from anyone who could tell it.

The elder prince said, 'You have been so kind and generous to me over the years. Do me one more favour, please. I would like to go and tell the king the story of my brother. Could you get me to the king's palace?'

The harissawala's daughter loved the elder prince dearly and agreed to help him. She smuggled him in the dead of night to the gate of the palace grounds. There, the elder prince told the gatekeeper that he

wanted to enter the palace and tell the king the story of his brother. In the morning, he was presented before the king. Neither recognised the other. Twelve years of hardship had aged the elder prince, while the younger prince had grown into a man, little resembling the little boy he had once been.

The elder prince began speaking, narrating the tale from the beginning, when their mother had summoned them to her deathbed till the point when the two brothers got separated. The king rose from his throne, ran to the elder prince, embraced him and began sobbing.

'I am the younger prince,' cried the king. 'I am your younger brother. I forgot for twelve long years that I even had a brother. The life of regal luxury acted as a blindfold, pushing all other thoughts away.'

The elder prince was also crying, and for a while the brothers held each other in a tight embrace. When they had calmed themselves a bit, the king offered his crown to the elder prince. 'You are older, the crown is yours by right,' he said. 'Please sit on the throne and rule this kingdom.' But the elder prince would not accept his younger brother's suggestion.

The king assumed the throne and asked that the harissawala be brought before him. He was tried and imprisoned for killing people and selling their flesh. The next order of business was to make the elder prince a minister in the king's court and to arrange his marriage with the harissawala's daughter.

The next thought in both their minds was to reunite with their father. The king sent people to his father's kingdom, and they came back with the news that their father had passed away; the wicked queen's son was ruling in his stead. The king had a strong army and decided that it was time to win back the kingdom which was rightfully theirs. Accordingly, the king invaded it, imprisoned the queen, killed her son and annexed the kingdom to his own.

The princes, now king and minister, lived together happily for the rest of their days.

Lotus seeds

'pʌmbʊchh - a tasty snack eaten raw, it is found after peeling many layers of the central part of a lotus before its flower petals form

The Daughter-in-Law Who Sulked

There was a household in which the daughter-in-law would often go into a huff. If something displeased her, or if someone said something that she did not like, she would turn away and sulk. She had to be cajoled for a long time before she would rejoin any family activities. In the beginning, it may have been oversensitivity that made her take offence so easily, but over time it became a habit. Also, as time passed, her sulks lasted much longer, testing her family's patience to the limit. When they asked her to get over this habit, she ignored them or took offence yet again.

One winter morning, she went into a sulk and stepped out of the house. It had snowed heavily overnight so instead of going outside the house, she stayed in the veranda, sitting with her bowed head held tight in her arms. She kept her eyes closed. Her family members looked at each other to see who would go first to coax her into a good mood and convince her to come back inside the house, for it was deathly cold.

When nobody seemed to offer to go first, her father-in-law said, 'Let's see how long she keeps it up and stays out in the cold if no one pays any attention to her.' The others voiced their enthusiastic agreement. They had all thought about just letting her sulk, but no one had had the courage to say it out loud until now. And so, they decided that there would be no cajoling today; she would come in when she herself felt like it.

When quite a bit of time had passed, the daughter-in-law began to wonder why no one had come to persuade her to go back inside. Suddenly, she heard footsteps and felt that someone was shaking her gently, wordlessly. 'Ah! Someone has come,' she thought with satisfaction.

Inside the house, her father-in-law also heard footsteps in the veranda. Then he heard his daughter-in-law say, 'No, I don't want to eat. I don't want to come. I will not enter the house. Go away. I've already told you I won't come. I want to stay here.' He wondered who had gone out to cajole her when they had all decided against doing so.

He stepped up to the window and was shocked to see that a large brown bear was in the veranda shaking his daughter-in-law's shoulder while she sat with her back to the animal, head down, talking away. The bear had seen her sitting so still that he wanted to check if she was alive before he ate her up. And now that she was speaking, he was confused.

The father-in-law's screams drew the entire household to the window. The minute they saw the bear, they grabbed sticks and started shouting and beating the sticks to scare it away. The bear was alarmed by the number of people around him and the noise they were making and ran away.

As for the daughter-in-law, she found her legs were shaking so much that she couldn't stand up. When someone finally helped her up and into the house, she had already made up her mind that she would never again go into a sulk.

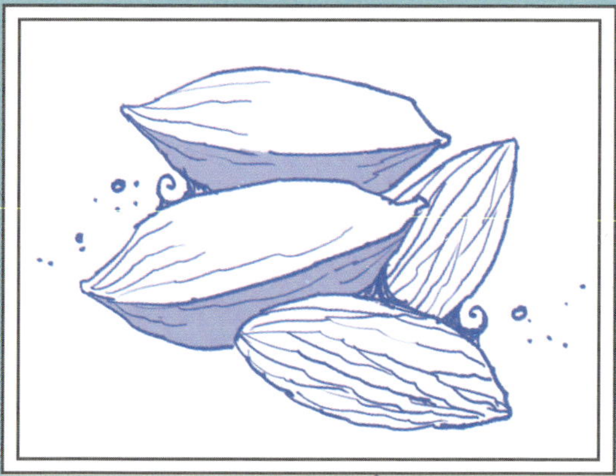

Green almond

'sʌbz ba:da:m - tender almond nuts are eaten before the skin hardens to a shell

The Gentleman and the Rogue

This tale takes place at a time when the only way for people to travel long distances was on foot, unless they owned a horse. One day, a man decided to go on a long journey so he put together some provisions and set out.

A few days later, he met another traveller who asked him, 'Who are you?'

'I am a decent, civilised man, a gentleman,' replied the man.

'"And where are you going?"

The gentleman named a place that would take a few months to reach. 'That's where I'm going. It's very far.'

The other man said, 'I would like to accompany you on the journey, because I like to travel.'

The gentleman agreed, and they began walking together. The gentleman asked his companion, 'Who are you?'

'I am a cunning man, a rogue,' he replied. 'I use my wile to get the better of others, and that makes me happy.'

'I am a decent man,' repeated the gentleman. 'I like to help people, and that is what makes me happy.'

They walked together companionably and sat down to rest when they were tired. The rogue told the gentleman, 'I'm thirsty.'

The gentleman got up and looked around. A river was flowing some distance away. He walked towards it and took off his cap, deciding to fill water in it for the rogue. The rogue, meanwhile, followed the gentleman stealthily. When the gentleman squatted by the river to fill his cap with water, the rogue rushed forward and gave him a mighty shove. The gentleman flailed desperately but could not find a handhold on any rock, and the undercurrent slowly dragged him into the depths of the river. The rogue ran back to where they had left their belongings, took all the gentleman's effects and provisions and set off, feeling very pleased with himself.

The gentleman was dragged down, down, deep into *patal*, where he found a house, which he entered. The house itself was strangely dry, though it was surrounded on all sides by water. It was a large house with many rooms; he hid in one and waited until he felt it was safe for him to go out. For a while, all he heard was the sound of the river lapping against the walls of the house. Then he heard two voices speaking in the next room.

The female voice said, 'Welcome home, my *dev*!'

The gentleman went rigid with shock. Not only was he in patal, he was actually inside the house of a dev!

The dev said, 'I have just returned from *zameen*, where the daughter of the king has an illness that no hakim is able to diagnose. But do you know, in the next room is a bottle of medicine, and it is the only bottle of medicine in the world that can cure the princess.'

The thought of the princess being unwell made the gentleman sad. She was the princess of the kingdom to which he belonged, and as a good citizen, it was his duty to help the king, who had always been kind and just in his rule. The gentleman looked around. The only place the medicine could be was inside a glass-fronted cabinet in the room. When he saw the bottle of medicine, he decided that he would take it to the princess so she could be healed. Praying to the Almighty to help him escape the dev's house without being discovered, he made his way outside quietly and began swimming up, towards the surface of the river.

The waters had receded greatly from the time when the rogue had pushed him in, so he soon reached the surface. After a few gulps of air, he swam to the riverbank. Thanking the Almighty for protecting him and checking to see that the bottle of medicine was safe in his pocket, he went towards the king's palace. He told the gatekeeper that he needed to see the king because he had with him the cure for the princess's illness. The audience hall was crowded with all manner of hakims and *tabibs*, and when it was the gentleman's turn, the king asked him, 'What medicine have you brought?'

He took the bottle out of his pocket and said, 'I have brought this medicine from across the seven seas and from the depths of the sea to cure the princess.'

The king, who had been losing hope of his daughter's recovery, signalled that the gentleman be allowed to administer the medicine to the princess. The moment the princess swallowed the medicine the gentleman offered her, she sat up, full of vitality. All signs of weakness and lassitude seemed to have vanished.

Overjoyed at her recovery, the king told the gentleman, 'My daughter owes her life to you. You are wise and knowledgeable. I would like to conduct a *nikah* between you and my daughter.' The gentleman agreed and became the son-in-law of the king. A few months later, the king decided that he had become too old to rule and abdicated the throne in favour of his son-in-law.

The gentleman, now the king, ruled wisely and well. One day, when he was on a *shikar*, he came across the rogue who had shoved him into the river. The rogue recognised the gentleman immediately. 'This is the man I threw in the river,' he thought. 'How come he's so richly dressed?' He decided to follow the gentleman and found himself at the gates of the palace. 'I'm an old friend of the king,' he told the gatekeeper. 'I'd like to meet him.'

The gatekeeper carried his message to the king, who summoned the rogue.

The rogue said, '*Badshah sahab*, I recognised you. I think we have met before.'

The king said, 'Yes, you are right. We have met before. You are the villain who pushed me into the river, aren't you?'

The rogue replied, 'Yes, Badshah sahab. I am that same rogue. But I know that you are a gentleman and you enjoy helping people.'

The king said, 'Yes, I have become the king, but I am still the same gentleman who likes to help people. Tell me, what do you want?'

The rogue asked, 'Tell me, how did you become the king? When I pushed you in the river, I thought that would be the end of you.'

The king narrated the entire story.

The rogue said, 'I would also like to be a king. Will you help me?'

'How can I help you?'

The rogue said, 'Please take me to the same spot on the same river and push me into it so that I too will find something in patal that will help me become a badshah.'

The king agreed to help the rogue. They left for the river, and when they reached the spot where the gentleman had squatted to fill water for the rogue, the king pushed the rogue into the river. The rogue also struggled against the water but was dragged under. He found the dev's house in patal, entered it and hid himself in a room. For a while, he heard the sound of water lapping against the walls of the house, but then he heard footsteps. It was the dev, entering the room where the rogue had hidden himself.

The dev said, 'Oh, have you come back to steal yet another bottle of my medicine? Wasn't it enough for you to have stolen it the first time around?' Saying this, he picked up the rogue and tore him into two.

And that was the end of the rogue, and it's also the end of our story.

Chinar

*tʃɪ'na:r*r - when leaves of the chinar tree fall in autumn and dry up, they are used as fuel in the kanger

How Some Kashmiri Surnames Were Formed

Giving people nicknames used to be a popular pastime in Kashmir. And often, those nicknames stuck and evolved to become surnames. People would identify something of note in a person and begin to call them that. Some people are called Khar, which means donkey. The people of a particular family had prominent buttocks—buttocks are called *mandul* in Kashmiri—and they were called by that name. The name stuck, and so you will find Manduloos in Kashmir, though they may not have prominent buttocks any more.

The story goes that there lived a man called Vishambar Nath. He had a magnificent tree in his garden. Since 'tree' is called *kul* in Kashmiri, people started calling him Vishambar Nath Kul. He asked them to refrain from adding the kul but nobody listened to him. Determined to get them to stop, he had the tree cut off, leaving only a stump. His wish was granted: people stopped adding kul to his name.

But they replaced it with *god*, which means ankle, since now the tree resembled a body with only the ankle and foot visible. Vishambar Nath God's irritation increased, and he decided to eliminate the root of the matter—literally, because he had the tree stump pulled out by its roots. It had been a magnificent tree. You can imagine how deep and wide its roots must have gone. When the stump was uprooted, there was no justification for people calling Vishambar Nath 'God', so they stopped doing so.

But the uprooted tree left a large ditch, *khod* in Kashmiri. He was promptly renamed Vishambar Nath Khod. Furious by now at the naming and renaming, he resolved to put the matter to rest. Summoning a gardener, he got the large ditch filled. It took a couple of days, but finally, it was done. The gardener, knowing that soil settles into the ground with time and rain, added a mound of soil to the ditch so that the ground would become level once it had settled. Vishambar Nath was relieved because people called him by his name without adding Khod to it.

However, when after a few months there was still a mound (though it was much smaller than it had been before) where the ditch had been, people started calling him *teng*, which means mound. At this point, Vishambar Nath gave up and became Vishambar Nath Teng. And you will find Kashmiris with the surname Teng even today.

* *Author's Note: For those who are wondering, there is no such origin story behind my surname.*

Acknowledgements

Deep gratitude to:

Red Panda publisher Vidhi Bhargava, who asked me if I'd like to retell Kashmiri folktales: the process has meant more to me than you will know. Saurabh Garge in Design, Shatrughan Pandey in Production and Divya Shah in Marketing: for bringing your special brand of magic to this book.

Illustrator extraordinaire Charbak Dipta.

Jameela Akhter, who told me many of these stories with verve and diligence: my deepest thanks, this book would not have been possible without you.

Khansa Kubra, who told me her mother was the perfect person to go to for Kashmiri folktales: she most certainly is. Thank you for your generosity and for sharing so much of yourself.

Mrs. Khem Lata Kachroo, who shared with me 'The Man Who Wanted to Be Rich'. Thank you!

My mother, Vijay Zutshi, who filled my childhood with the shenanigans of characters she made up. My father, M.K. Zutshi, who recently told me *How Some Kashmiri Surnames Were Formed*, and helped me get the nuance of Koshur words right. Pa, Ma: thank you both, for more than I can even know, for without you, I would not be.

My sister Monica, to whom this book is dedicated, was instrumental in connecting me with Khansa: thank you for more than you can know, for walking behind me, ahead of me, and beside me.

My daughter Jailekha: thank you for choosing me. I am in awe of who you are.

You, dear reader: when we lose stories, we lose parts of ourselves. The tragedy is that we do not recognise the hollows this loss leaves. Thank you for reaching for this book–I hope it fills you up.

Glossary

aap char: you four

agar pachhin: a large, strong mythical bird of prey (similar to the roc of Sinbad's Tales)

arre: an expression of surprise

Badshah: king, but also a way to address a king

bhaisahab: brother, often used as a way to address a male stranger

chatai: floor mat used for sitting or lying down

dev: djinn

dhol: drum

fakir: a person (usually male) who has renounced the world for religion and lives on the charity of others

ghunghat: veil

god: ankle

hakim: a doctor who practises herbal medicine

haldi: turmeric

harissawala: a man who sells harissa, a traditional

dish of ground meat and grains cooked slowly, usually eaten for breakfast

jamadari: association

khala / khala jaan: aunt (mother's sister) / dear aunt

khar: donkey

khod: ditch

khwaja: a rich man

kul: tree

mandul: buttocks

meher: the wealth (gold, money, cattle, land, etc.) given by the bridegroom to his wife-to-be so she has money of her own

meher uthana: a ritual in which the husband's mother lifts the veil of her daughter-in-law for the first time after the newlyweds come home. The mother-in-law sees her daughter-in-law's face for the first time and gives her a gift, usually jewellery or money

nikah: marriage ceremony

pari: fairy / paris: fairies

patal: the netherworld, where devs and paris live

pheran: a loose, woollen coat of knee length or longer, worn by both men and women as the outermost layer of clothing. In severe winters, people would keep little baskets of live coals inside their pherans to keep their body warm

phuphi: aunt (father's sister)

rantas: a fictitious female character in Kashmiri folklore, she has long hair she wears loose to hide her face. She can take the form of any person, and lures people to entrap and then eat them. Her feet are reversed and toes point backwards, so she is usually careful to keep her feet hidden

sahab: sir

saraf: silversmith

shal: jackal

shikar: hunt

tabib: doctor

tanga: horse-drawn carriage

teng: mound

zameen: earth

zamindar: landowner who rents his land to farmers who till the soil and grow crops